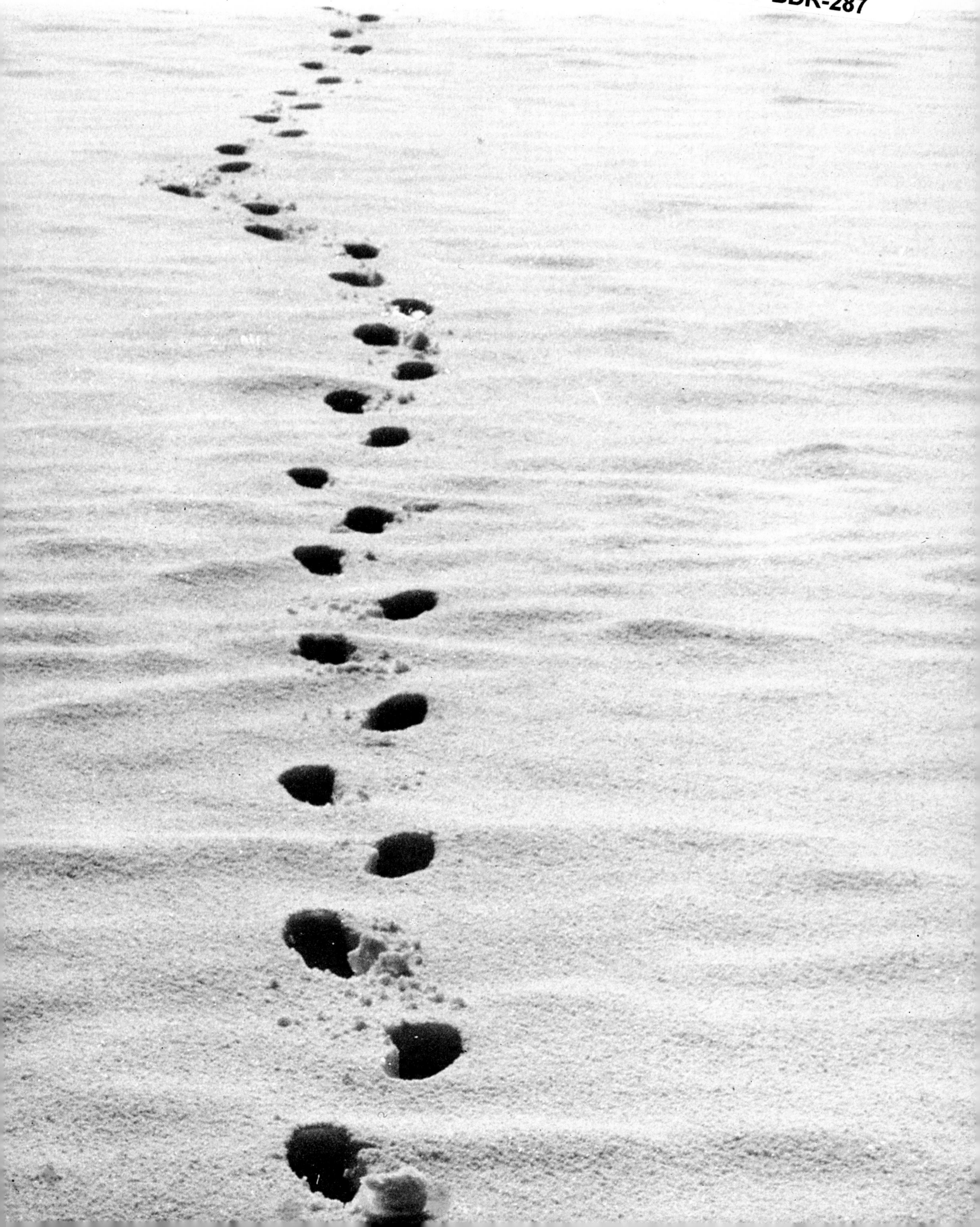

A BOOK OF BELIEFS

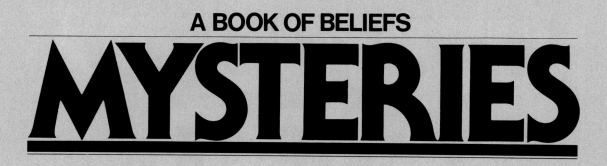

MYSTERIES

JOHN ALLAN

David C. Cook Publishing Co.

ELGIN, ILLINOIS—WESTON, ONTARIO

Published in the United States by
David C. Cook Publishing Co.
850 N. Grove, Elgin, IL 60120
ISBN: 0 89191 477 3

Library of Congress Catalog Card No. LC 81–67764
All rights reserved.
First United States edition 1981

Published in the United Kingdom by
Lion Publishing
Icknield Way, Tring, Herts, England
ISBN: 0 85648 318 4

Published in Australia by
Albatross Books
PO Box 320, Sutherland, NSW 2232, Australia
ISBN: 0 86760 260 0

First edition 1981

Printed by New Interlitho SPA, Italy

The photographs in this book are reproduced by
permission of the following photographers and
organizations:
Barnaby's Picture Library 41(right), 55, 58–59(below)
Camera Press 18–19, 34–35(centre)
John H. Cutten 22–23(above), 25(right)
Daily Telegraph Picture Library 15(right)
Barry Kirk 16–17
Mary Evans Picture Library 23 (above),30–31(below),
44–45(centre); Harry Price Collection (Universiy of
London) 34(left), 48(left), 59(above); Society for
Psychical Research 26–27
Fortean Picture Library 6(left), 7(right), 8–9(both), 48–
49(right), 50–51
Alan Hutchison Library 36–37
Keystone Press 24–25(centre), 46–47(both), 57
Frank Lane Picture Library 6–7(centre)
Lion Publishing: Jon Willcocks cover, title pages, 2–3,
4–5, 10–11, 38–39, 42–43(both)
Mansell Collection 12–13, 44(left), 56
Linda Mindel 28–29
Popperfoto 20–21(centre), 35(right), 60–61
Science Photo Library 14–15(below and centre)
Souvenir Press 54(left)
Syndication International 40–41(centre)
The Times Picture Library 32–33
John Topham Picture Library 19(right), 21(below), 30(above),
33(right), 52–53, 54(right)

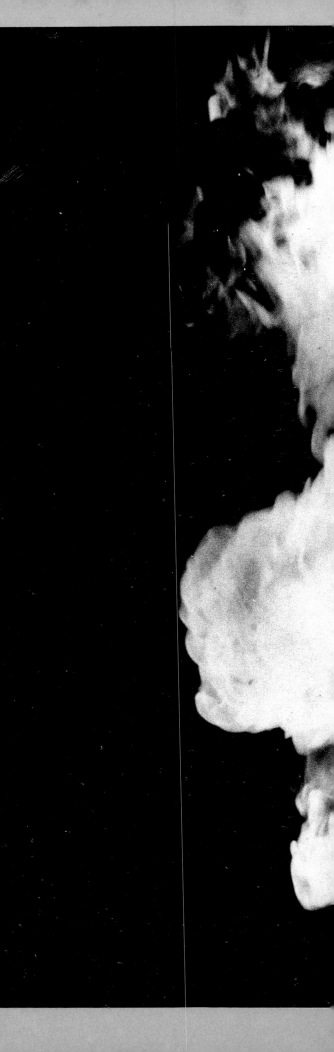

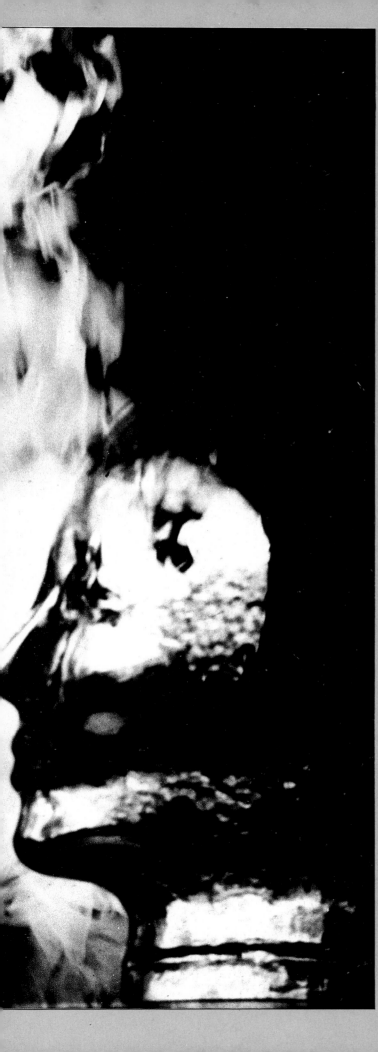

CONTENTS

MYSTERIES

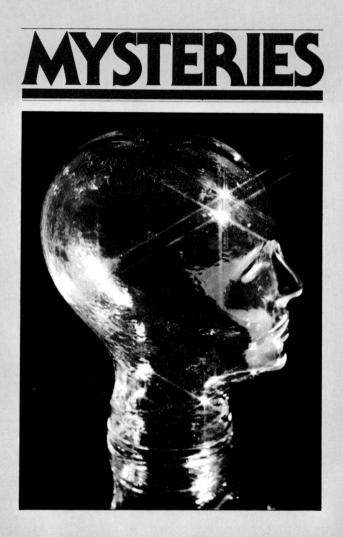

INTRODUCING MYSTERIES

Skulls that scream ... heavy tables rising in the air ... strange craft in the skies ... people who suddenly burst into flames. The subject matter of this book is exciting and exotic. It is also vast. All that we can do here is to draw the main outlines of the paranormal, to give the briefest of introductions to a subject which is frequently complex, baffling and very contradictory.

And please remember, as you read, that in this area there are more dubious and fraudulent claims per square inch than in almost any other subject. There are several reasons for being cautious.

Deliberate faking

The nineteenth-century fascination with spirit messages began on 31 March 1848, when three young girls—Kate, Margaret and Leah Fox—discovered they were receiving mysterious communications, in rapping noises, from a 'spirit' who claimed to be a murdered pedlar. Or were they?

In 1888 Margaret Fox publicly admitted that it had been 'all fraud, hypocrisy and delusion'. Was this a genuine confession, or was she just an embittered widow, envious of the fame of her successful sister Leah? One thing is sure: since 1848, there has been no lack of fraudulent mediums who have faked 'supernatural' noises and apparitions in order to make money.

Inaccurate reporting

Erich von Däniken's theory that human beings were 'created' by astronauts has won him 35 million readers. Few of them realize that his six books are simply a tissue of inaccuracies and factual distortions.

When a theory is attractive, people are often careless about facts. In 1915 Arthur Machen wrote a story 'entirely without foundation' about angel troops who had rescued British soldiers in the retreat from Mons. To his horror, the story was accepted as true, and several 'witnesses' of the angels came forward. The legend still lingers today.

Auto-suggestion

When it suits their wishes, people are often prone to believe what appears to happen rather than what does. And this can produce real effects.

Australian 'clever men', for example, perform psychic 'operations' on the bodies of sick believers. Ronald Rose once asked one of them if it wasn't just clever conjuring. 'Smiling, he agreed, but immediately stressed the psychological point of view: "They bin get better all the same."'

A mixture of causes

The famous Cock Lane ghost in Smithfield, London, in 1759 was probably a genuine paranormal occurrence. But no one would believe this when Elizabeth, the daughter of the house, was detected counterfeiting rapping noises with a piece of board. However, Elizabeth had been told that unless the ghost manifested itself that night, her family would be sent to prison; and so probably she simply decided to lend a helping hand. She could certainly not have counterfeited some of the other manifestations. In this way paranormal phenomena, genuine in origin, can become entangled with purely human effects.

Demonic deception

The Bible teaches that there is a deceptive, dangerous spirit world which human beings should make no attempt to contact, which distorts reality and can ruin lives.

Many paranormal researchers have become aware of the reality of something evil behind the phenomena which they investigate. G.K. Chesterton commented, after experimenting with a ouija board, 'The only thing I will say with complete confidence, about that mystic and invisible power, is that it tells lies.'

The paranormal is real; there is too much evidence to dismiss it as wishful thinking. But it is not necessarily nice; and never straightforward.

Investigating mysteries

We are living at a time in history when science seems to be demonstrating, over and over again, how little we know about reality. Quantum physics, DNA, genetic codes, quasars—all of these revolutionary new ideas 'represent not only additions to *what man knows* but changes in *the way he knows*'. This claim is made by Professor Harold Schilling, an American physicist. He continues, 'Men's minds and hearts are being liberated from inhibiting attitudes and conceptions . . . they are now able to explore realms and dimensions of reality from which they had been blocked until recently.'

Is there a supernatural? Are there paranormal powers and agencies of which science has so far failed to take account? This book will show that there are many areas in which there is some evidence that we still have massive discoveries to make. But there is evidence, too, of real perils and deceptions, and it is hoped that the book will serve as a warning as well as an explanation. I write this book from my position as a committed Christian. And I hope that by the end you will see that such a standpoint is not a blinkered one; rather it offers our only hope of understanding the world of the paranormal in a sane and safe way.

JOHN ALLAN

TIME AND SPACE

Einstein's theories have fundamentally changed our understanding of time and space. Do they also provide the key to some extraordinary mysteries?

Nobody believed Sister Mary when she told her superiors about her work in converting the Jumano Indians to Christianity. It was hardly surprising. The Indians were in Central America—and her convent was in Spain.

But then Father Alonzo de Benavides returned from Mexico in 1630, bringing stories of a mysterious 'lady in blue' who had visited several areas to evangelize before him. He brought with him a chalice which the lady had left behind; and it was recognized as coming from Mary's convent. When she was questioned on obscure points of Indian lore and Mexican geography, her knowledge proved phenomenal. Yet she had never left Spain for a second.

Materializations and teleporting

Can a person be in two places simultaneously? The pupils of nineteenth-century teacher Emilie Sagée certainly thought so. On one occasion, when Emilie was writing on the blackboard, her double appeared beside her. At another time she 'materialized' in a classroom when the real Emilie was clearly visible outside in the garden. Two of the girls who touched the apparition said it felt like muslin'; another boldly walked through her.

Telepathy is a possible explanation of some cases like this. Sometimes apparitions can be projected telepathically into the minds of other people, and their minds will then be stimulated to produce a recognizable image of the 'agent'. It has been shown that this image will act naturally and usually obey physical laws (such as producing reflections in a mirror), sometimes communicating verbally.

But this does not explain Sister Mary's very solid chalice. Fanciful elaboration? Perhaps; 1630 was a long time ago.

But there may be other explanations. Albert Einstein held that motion affected time and distance. For example, a spaceship travelling at half the speed of light would be only 85 per cent of its length when at rest, and the clock on board would be running at only 85 per cent of its normal rate. He saw space–time as a unity, rather than two entities, 'space' and 'time', which suggests that it might have more flexible qualities than we have imagined.

Perhaps, occasionally, it is possible for time and space to become compressed in such a way that the normal rules no longer apply. That might explain why a honeymoon couple in Brazil felt drowsy as they drove in Rio Grade do Sul, fell asleep—and woke up in Mexico!

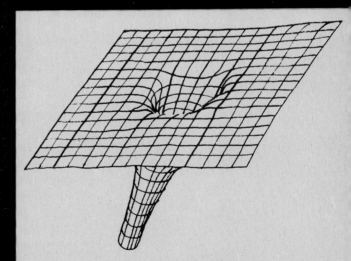

BLACK HOLES

The normal laws of time and space are dramatically flouted by 'black holes'. These form in space when a star burns up all of its internal energy and collapses in on itself, with a stronger and stronger gravitational pull, until it becomes infinitesimally small. It soaks up all light, allowing none to escape, and so becomes invisible; it sucks nearby objects into itself, crushing them to nothing, and inside its 'event horizon' (sucking distance) time operates differently. Some scientists suggest that travellers drawn into a black hole will emerge on the other side, through a 'white hole', into another dimension; this is unproven.

Professor John Taylor's best-seller *Black Holes: The End of the Universe?* argues that the discovery of black holes shatters all of our religious conceptions. His argument is based on a series of naive assumptions and misunderstandings of basic Christian teaching (for example, about soul and mind, Satan and the Fall, the personality of God, salvation and immortality). Interestingly, his colleague R.L.F. Boyd—Head of the Mullard Space Science Laboratory, concerned in the discovery of black holes—is an unabashedly convinced Christian.

DEFYING SCIENCE

In Singapore in 1861 an earthquake was followed by a deluge of rain. After the rain, the streets were full of fish. Where had they come from?

Do showers of frogs fall out of the sky? Can rain be black, or yellow, or red? How can we explain metal objects found inside lumps of coal, or the gopher turtle who flopped out of the clouds into a small Mississippi village?

Charles Fort's third book, *Lo!*, was published in 1931. It described many strange events, but suggested no explanations. Fort said, 'I shall find out for myself, and anyone who cares to, may find out with me.'

Fort and Forteana

Questions like these fascinated the peculiar brain of Charles Hoy Fort. A penniless journalist from a wealthy New York family, Fort devoted his life to collecting facts which would not fit into nineteenth-century science. He wrote seven unreadable books, but is mainly remembered for his third, *The Book of the Damned* (1919), which pieces together a weird array of facts 'damned' by scientists who could not explain them.

Although not much recognized in his lifetime, Fort has many modern-day admirers, and a Fortean Society still catalogues in its *Fortean Times* strange information from around the world. Fort had no theory about why these odd occurrences took place (although he suggested several); he simply wanted to expose the smugness of scientific orthodoxy. Recently *The*

Book of the Damned has begun selling widely again. 'Forteana'—the kind of phenomena which delighted Fort—have continued unabated throughout this century. In January 1969 in Maryland, hundreds of dead ducks dropped on to the streets; in June 1954, hundreds of little frogs bounced off the heads of pedestrians in crowded streets in Birmingham.

Strange abilities continue to be shown by unlikely people; Ted Serios, for example, a simple-minded alcoholic hotel worker from Chicago, has developed the ability to produce identifiable pictures ('thoughtographs') on a piece of photographic film, simply by staring into the camera lens. As he places a 'gismo'—a cardboard tube—against the lens first, there have been allegations of fakery, but Serios has performed his feats under stringent test conditions.

No one knows what ball lightning is. A small bright globule generally follows an erratic course, sometimes passing through walls, or even aeroplanes in flight, before exploding.

Spontaneous combustion

One of the most gruesome phenomena investigated by Fort was 'spontaneous

On 5 December 1966 the gasman called on Dr John Irving Bentley, a semi-invalid who lived on his own in Pennsylvania, USA. When he got no reply to his calls, he searched the house and found this gruesome sight; a mysterious fire had totally consumed Dr Bentley, but damaged nothing around him.

combustion'. Mrs Mary Carpenter was on a boating holiday in East Anglia, in the summer of 1938, when suddenly she burst into flames and was reduced to ashes in front of her husband and children. They were unharmed, and so was the boat. There was no flame from which she could have caught fire.

She was one of about two dozen known cases of 'spontaneous combustion' in the last hundred years. Strangely, the surroundings of 'combustion' cases are usually unaffected by the flames; in 1922 Mrs Euphemia Johnson's calcined bones were found lying in a heap inside her undamaged clothes. The explanation may be something to do with the effect of magnetic disturbances upon the body (many cases happen within a weak magnetic field) or the electrical discharge of the human body itself.

WHAT IS THE WORLD?

Some people think that the miracles recounted in the Bible contravene natural laws, and therefore cannot be true. But this is to misunderstand what natural laws are.

The word 'law' can mean two things: first, a *prescription* for human conduct (for instance, 'You must not steal or you will be sent to prison'); second, a *description* of what seems to be happening in nature or scientific experiments. 'Natural laws' are descriptions of what we observe taking place around us, not prescriptions for what *must* happen! When we see something occurring which seems to conflict with the natural laws we understand (for instance, an aeroplane in the sky, which

conflicts with the laws of gravity) it does not mean *either* that the law of gravity does not work *or* that our senses are deceiving us; it simply means that there are other natural laws at work which we may not know about (in this case, the laws of aerodynamics).

Hence the Bible's miracles need not be suspensions of natural laws (although if God is really the all-powerful Creator, there is no reason why they shouldn't be). Both miracles and Forteana could *also* simply be applications of natural principles we do not yet understand. Indeed, the Bible stresses that the universe does not operate randomly, but is created and sustained in an ordered way by God.

THE UNKNOWN EARTH

Lines of power. Dragon paths. Did our ancestors understand the world we live in better than we do?

On 30 June 1921, an English brewer named Alfred Watkins was riding across the hills of Herefordshire. As he looked down on the countryside below, he suddenly realized that the little churches, the hilltops and the ancient monuments seemed to fall into a pattern. It was as though there had once been a system of straight lines and tracks connecting them.

Leys

Watkins expanded his ideas into a book. He claimed that the tracks, which he called 'ley lines', were a system of ancient trade routes running right across Britain. Not many archaeologists were convinced, but later Wilhelm Teudt found identical tracks—'heilige Linien'—in Germany, and Xavier Guichard claimed to trace an amazing geodetic system running right across Europe and linking up hundreds of towns with names sounding like 'Alesia' (Versailles, Alessio, Calais, Elsendorf). In the locality of each one, he claimed, one could find landscaped hills and a man-made well.

It seems impossible that leys were trade routes. But dowsers such as Guy Underwood have suggested that the connection with water is important. Megalithic sites (see *Ancient Engineering*) seem at times to contain a mysterious energy, not unlike electromagnetism, and it is possible that the leys were channels for flows of this energy. Underwood suggests that the underground springs at ancient sites have something to do with the 'geodetic force' which he has discovered there. Certainly both Stonehenge and Avebury may be criss-crossed by a labyrinthine network of underground streams, and Welsh dowser Bill Lewis claims to sense a spiral force around ancient standing stones, derived from the streams which cross one another directly under the stone.

Was there once an age when men lived closer to the earth than today, and so knew of strange forces running through the earth which are presently unknown to science? In China it is still common to site new buildings carefully according to the laws of *feng-shui*, an intricate code for fitting buildings into landscapes in harmony with the 'earth force', observing 'dragon paths' which, like leys, run across the land. Most scientists still doubt that 'geodetic force' has any reality; but no really satisfactory testing has yet been done.

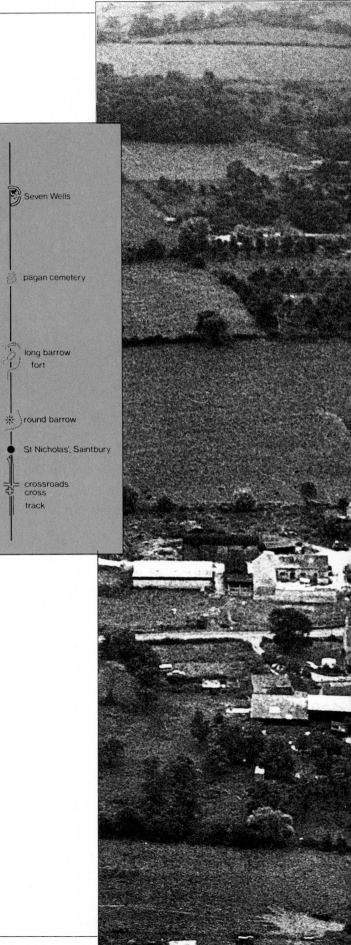

Seven Wells

pagan cemetery

long barrow
fort

round barrow

St Nicholas', Saintbury

crossroads
cross

track

N

A typical alignment of man-made sites is the so-called Saintbury ley in the west of England. In a three-and-a-half-mile straight line lie an old cross, a road, a church and four ancient earthworks.

Geometric earth?

Three Russian scientists of the sixties—scholars of history, engineering and electronics—combined to write a paper for the USSR Academy of Sciences, entitled *Is the Earth a Huge Crystal?* They believe it is possible to trace a lattice-work pattern, a 'matrix of cosmic energy', running across the earth's face, dividing it into twelve pentagonal slabs.

They claim that the idea explains the siting of ancient civilizations, the occurrence of hurricanes, volcanoes, and magnetic anomalies. Western scientists are less convinced; they point out that the supposed 'lines' are drawn so vaguely that anything could be read into them; and that if it is true that the continents have shifted position, the 'crystalline' symmetry would have disappeared long ago.

A HOLLOW EARTH?

When Charles Fort (see *Defying Science*) theorized in his book *Y* that the earth could perhaps be hollow, no one paid any attention. But recently the idea has surfaced again, notably in the books of Brinsley Le Poer Trench, one of Britain's foremost UFO experts and a member of the House of Lords. Trench believes that:

● We are being watched from the skies by a friendly race of space visitors.

● We are also being threatened from within by another evil race.

● This race lives inside the hollow earth and reaches the surface via a crater at the North Pole.

● Photographs of the earth from space often show a strange indentation over the Pole—the crater lip.

Quite apart from the fact that to Trench, Jesus is merely an 'initiate', not the Son of God, there seems to be overwhelming evidence against his point of view.

TAPPING NATURAL FORCES

*Metal detectors are a useful tool in looking for buried treasure.
But many claim that a piece of hazel twig would do just as well.*

Where does water come from? There is something like 1,370 million cubic kilometres of it in the oceans of the world—far too much simply to have dropped from the sky as rain. Scientists are beginning to think that somehow water is formed somewhere deep within the earth—at the rate of 100 cubic metres per year.

Finding underground water

Whether or not this is true, it is something which 'dowsers' have always believed. Dowsing is the art of tracking down underground sources of water with the help of a forked twig—preferably of peach, hazel, willow or witch-hazel, but whalebone or wire can do instead. Dowsing has been practised for centuries, and often works when orthodox geology fails. But no one knows how it works. Is it simply a response to natural laws we have yet to discover, or is some supernatural force involved?

If it is a purely natural process, it is hard to explain why it works when the fork is held above a map of an area, as well as in the area itself. And certainly an interest in dowsing has led some gifted, sensitive practitioners into an unhealthy fascination with other 'supernatural' practices. But many dowsers are practical, unspeculative people more concerned with employing their gift

usefully than with occult study. Perhaps they are simply more sensitive than others to a kind of radiation signal emitted by the stream. But then again it is possible to dowse for other things besides water; dowsing can become a kind of clairvoyance.

Beyond water

Dowsers claim that some underground water—'black streams'—can trigger off arthritis and cancer in human beings. Dr Herbert Douglas of Vermont was sceptical about this. But when he tested the beds, chairs and couches of 55 arthritic patients, he found that without exception they were placed above the intersection of underground streams. Twenty-five of the patients agreed to move to a different bed—and each of them either improved condition or was completely cured.

Dowsing becomes dangerous when the practitioner moves from exploring real, if mysterious, phenomena in the physical world, to making unwarranted assumptions about the supernatural. Tom Lethbridge, for example, who dowsed with a pendulum, came to believe that beyond a certain length the pendulum registered vibrations from another 'dimension'—the world beyond death. There are no grounds for this idea.

THE FINDHORN COMMUNITY

At Findhorn in the North of Scotland there is a 'New Age community' which boasts unusual agricultural achievements. On fairly unpromising soil the community members have grown plants of staggering size in spectacular profusion. They attribute their success to the fact that they have attuned themselves to the energies and forces of nature, and are guided by communications from Devas (the spirits of plants) and Nature Spirits (elves, gnomes and fairies,

including the god Pan, all of whom are 'servants of God and function according to His will only'). Spirit messages and visions are important.

Some outsiders attribute their successes to collective ESP, and dismiss the 'spirits' as delusions; but in view of the way in which the 'spirit' messages have drawn the community from a broadly Christian base deeper and deeper into pagan nature-worship, it is possible that demonic forces are also at work.

DISAPPEARANCES

A few days' journey from Japan, nine ships disappeared without trace in four years. A government ship was sent to investigate. It disappeared.

It was 7 November 1872, when Captain David Moorhouse of the *Dei Gratia* spotted another ship behaving erratically just ahead. They were in the Atlantic, some 600 miles/950 km west of Gibraltar. It looked as if no one was steering the other ship. With a shock, he realized she was the *Mary Celeste*—a ship with a 'jinx' reputation, commanded by his friend Benjamin Briggs. Fearing the worst for Briggs, Moorhouse hurriedly sent across a boarding party. They found—nothing.

From that moment on, the *Mary Celeste* was destined to become the best-known mystery ship of all time. Where were the Briggs family and the crew of eight? There were no signs of violence. Oliver Deveau, leader of the boarding party, later testified, 'There seemed to be everything left behind in the cabins as if left in a great hurry, but everything in its place.'

What happened? We may never know; none of the many theories quite fit the facts. All we can say is that many theories cannot be disproved. There is certainly no case for suspecting intervention by astronauts or flying saucers. Strange things happen at sea, and paranormal causes should never be invoked until natural ones have been ruled out.

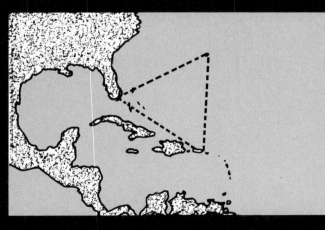

The Bermuda Triangle
Most people have heard of the 'Bermuda Triangle', first described by Vincent Gaddis in 1964. 'This relatively limited area,' he claimed, 'is the scene of disappearances that total far beyond the laws of chance.'

Unfortunately, the US Coastguard Service announce that very few ships do disappear in the

MANIPULATING DISAPPEARANCES

Why do things (and people) disappear? One suggestion is that gravitational or magnetic forces can be tampered with artificially. Maurice Jessup claimed in 1955 that the US Navy had actually done this 12 years earlier—rendering a destroyer and its crew invisible, and 'teleporting' them from Philadelphia to the area of Newport News.

Although the experiment was a success, according to Jessup, the crew suffered terribly; some died and others went insane. The 'Philadelphia Experiment' has become a well-known legend, but unfortunately it seems never to have happened. Jessup was relying on shoddy information.

It may not be impossible, in principle, for something like this to happen; but we cannot say. It has never been done, and we know too little about magnetic properties to attempt it.

Triangle. In 1975, for instance, of 21 ships lost without trace off the American coastline, only four were in the Triangle. There is also a question as to where the Triangle *is*; if the corners of it are Florida, Bermuda and Puerto Rico, then most of the tragedies claimed for it actually happened outside.

Lawrence Kusche of Arizona State University has shown definitively that most of the legendary Triangle mysteries can be explained quite simply. The best one can say is that this area of the world is prone to sudden freak storms, and magnetic irregularities, which can sometimes lead to inexplicable disasters.

The Marie Celeste case is one of the world's best-known mysteries.

MYSTERIES OF THE BODY

From time to time, as medical knowledge increases, doctors are forced to take seriously ideas that had been dismissed as old wives' tales.

In 1939 Soviet doctor Semyon Kirlian made a strange discovery. When he placed his hand between two electrodes containing a photographic plate, and turned on the current, he found that he had produced a photograph—not just of his hand, but also of a strange glowing aura around it.

Experiments showed that leaves, and other people's hands, produced the same results. The colour and type of aura seemed to vary depending on whether or not the person was well, sick, or mentally disturbed. Was this a new discovery about the human body? Are we all surrounded by a Kirlian aura?

Earlier, in 1911, Walter J. Kilner of St Thomas's Hospital had discovered that he could see an 'envelope of energy' surrounding human bodies when he looked at them through a solution of dicyanin diluted in alcohol. This envelope, he claimed, consisted of three layers— an outer and inner aura, and the 'etheric double'—which radiated for 12 inches/30 cm from the body and changed in size and colour when the person was sick or hypnotized.

A useful study?

Disciples of Kilner have since discovered a type of glass reportedly producing the same results as dicyanin, and 'Kirlian goggles' are now available for sale. Scientists are sceptical; it is possible that the 'auras' (which not everyone can see) are produced simply by suggestion. Kirlian photography is equally unproven. Some results could have been examples of 'Lichtenburg figures', a well-known electrical phenomenon which has nothing to do with the human aura. Professor William Tiller has shown since that there were many potential sources of uncontrolled error in Kirlian's research equipment, and that when the equipment was stringently controlled there were no differences between the auras of different types.

Kirlian's advocates point out that Tiller is now admitting that 'some of the conclusions . . . may have been premature', and that his work was based only on the fingertips, not the whole hand. But their case is far from proven.

Acupuncture

For centuries the Chinese have taught that the body is crossed by lines of force, the junctions of

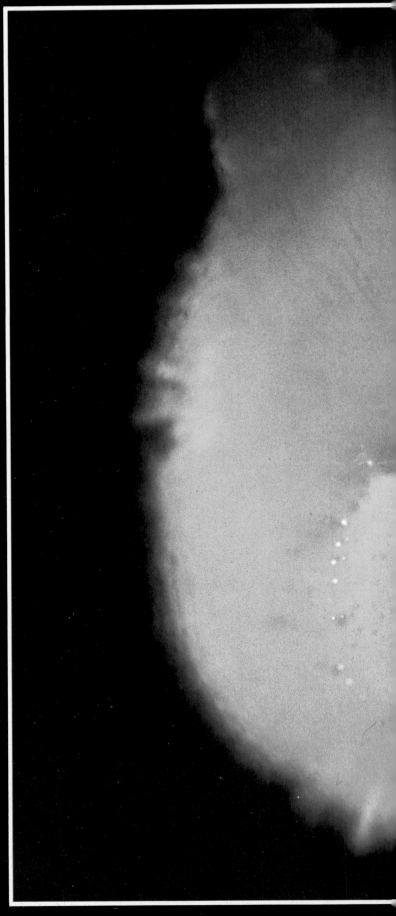

This is the glow not of a gas-ring but of a human fingertip! Living organisms have a faint electrical current around them, and the technique of Kirlian photography enables this to be seen. Some practitioners claim that changing moods are made visible by the Kirlian photographs and analyse them in the same way as palm-reading.

which control bodily health. This is the basis for acupuncture, the science of inserting vibrating needles at the junction points in order to induce anaesthesia or even a cure. Recently a Christian doctor, Meg Patterson, has introduced electro-acupuncture to Britain as a seemingly effective cure for drug addictions; however, she has found that a slight electrical charge—without the insertion of needles—has an equal effect. The scientific validity of acupuncture has yet to be properly examined in the West, but undeniably it has achieved interesting results, and is used regularly in medicine and surgery in the East.

There is much we have yet to discover about our bodies; perhaps, just perhaps, some of these experimental techniques may point the way forward. But we need more evidence.

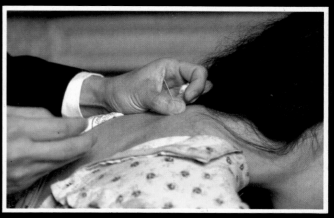

Acupuncture has been practised for centuries in China, but it is only recently that it has been used in the West.

WHAT IS MANKIND?

The expression and development of bodily powers is often seen as a path to spiritual enlightenment. But the Bible's view is that more than personal development is needed.

● Some religions, such as Hinduism, teach that there is no distinction between the physical and spiritual aspects of man. Therefore, bodily practices such as meditation, yoga exercises or chanting can help us realize God within ourselves.

● Other points of view, deriving from Platonic philosophy, hold that the body is unspiritual and therefore evil. The only way to realize God is to loathe and mistreat the body.

● Christians have at times been influenced by both these views. But the Bible's emphasis is rather different. God created man. All that God created is good. Therefore man's body is good. But man is more than body—he is also spirit. And only when made spiritually alive by contact with Jesus Christ does he become capable of appreciating and knowing God.

HEALING

All over the world, alternative medicine is practised. What powers enable people to heal the sick?

On 7 October every year, the *Liverpool Echo* carries a special notice. It is a message of gratitude from Mrs Sheila Speirs to the man who gave her back her health; and she intends to insert it every year until she dies. The man concerned is not a doctor, but an ex-blacksmith from Liverpool called John Cain.

Cain has been a full-time healer since 1972. He is one of around 8,000 spiritual healers in the British Isles, 2,500 of whom belong to a body known as the National Federation of Spiritual Healers. This body is gradually attracting more attention and interest from the medical profession.

In Brazil, spirit healing has always been more respectable. There has been a 600-bed Spirit Hospital there since 1926. In Britain, the Medical Association claims that no one has conclusively shown that spiritual healers do any good. But in 1977 the General Medical Council permitted doctors to refer patients to healers provided they kept control of the case. Before this, any doctor doing so would have been struck off the register.

What happens?

Spirit healers work in a variety of ways. Cain often lays hands on clients, but has also found that the very sight of his picture can trigger off healing. Once he instructed a lady by telephone to place her hands on a sick nephew's head; working as Cain's proxy, she was able to cure the boy.

Healing seems to involve a transfer of energy from one person to the other. Harry Edwards, the famous psychic healer, used to close his eyes to attune himself and feel the power flowing through him, before he would do anything. But exactly what the energy *is*, it would be hard to say.

It is also hard to establish when a genuine cure has taken place; all sorts of factors can be at work. 'Spontaneous remission', for example (when a disease abates of its own accord) can happen unpredictably for no apparent reason. Wrong diagnosis is another possibility which can account for an unexpected change in a patient's condition.

How does it happen?

Though some healing can be explained away, there seem to be real successes. Why? Many healers believe that their powers come from spirit guides with medical skills. Matthew Manning

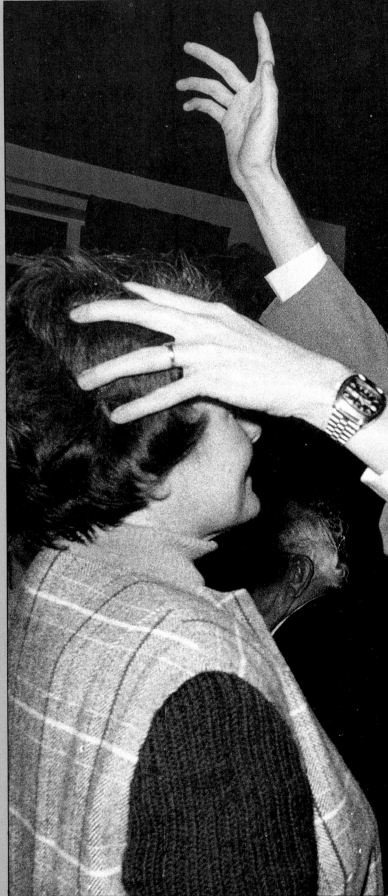

One of Britain's best-known healers is Trevor Dearing. A Christian minister, he received the power to heal at the time of a personal spiritual renewal. His work is now entirely devoted to exercising what he sees as an important gift from God.

produces by automatic writing diagnoses from a nineteenth-century doctor who calls himself Thomas Penn; these diagnoses have often proved fantastically correct. On the other hand, some of them have merely fulfilled the subconscious fantasies of the patient, clearly because Manning has picked up telepathic messages from them. Manning himself is very sceptical about whether his powers prove survival after death.

'Gifts of healings' are mentioned in the Bible as a spiritual attribute given by the Holy Spirit to some Christians. But that does not rule out the possibility that some people, too, may have natural gifts of healing which science cannot at this moment explain. The danger is that their gifts may lead them into wrong ideas about the nature of the supernatural world; few are as objective as Manning. There is also the possibility that Satan can produce 'counterfeit gifts' for purposes of deceit; Jesus warned that any of his miracles was liable to be copied by the powers of evil.

Spirit surgery

In Brazil and the Philippines, there are spirit healers who claim to open up bodies with their bare hands, remove diseased matter, and then cause the wound to heal over instantly, leaving no scar. At times this is mere conjuring; the growths supposedly removed have proved to be decayed chicken livers. Jim Jones, fanatical leader of the mass-suicide 'People's Temple' cult, used to produce such 'miracle cures' by sleight of hand.

The British scientist Lyall Watson, who has watched spirit healers in action, is convinced that some are 'capable of controlled materializations'. In other words, the objects removed do not come from within the patient's body, but simply appear at the healer's fingertips.

What must be said is that whenever exhaustive tests have been done, there has always been plenty of evidence of fraud. 'Spirit cures' are often psychosomatic, brought about by the patient's faith in the healer, not by the healer's actions themselves.

Types of healing

There are probably four types of 'miraculous' healing which need to be distinguished. *Spirit healing* is practised by witch doctors and shamans, who place themselves at the use of spirit powers in general, without any clear idea of which spirits are using them. *Spiritual healing* involves the summoning of certain known spirits to provide the power required. Harry Edwards, for instance, used to call on the power of Louis Pasteur. *Psychic healing* is manifested quietly and unspectacularly by a few people who claim to have had the ability since birth. Seemingly, there is no spirit involvement. *Christian 'gifts of healing'* are given by the Holy Spirit to some Christians.

All four types can work. The only question is: what precisely is the supernatural agency which is supplying the mysterious power to heal?

HOLISTIC HEALTH

'Holism' or 'holistic health' is the name given to the movement (centred on America) which is promoting in hospitals and universities the viability of 'non-traditional means of treatment' in healing disease. This includes psychic surgery, bio-energetic therapy, radionics, laying on of hands, and 'soul therapy'.

Some of these techniques are arguably effective, but there are two problems: first, little thought is given to *how* they work, and so we may not be aware of *all* their effects; second, holism often involves unjustified religious stances. 'Holistic Health is a point of view about the Universe,' according to one spokesman; '. . . the creative intention . . . leads each person to . . . seek a personal knowledge of the inner vision and spirit of the Higher Self (God within).'

By contrast, Christians believe that God is external to us, and can be personally known only by someone who enters into a relationship with him through Jesus Christ.

YOGA

'Yoga' is the Hindu word which signifies a spiritual discipline by which men may reach union with God. Thus it covers a wide range of religious practices. What most Westerners know as 'yoga' is one branch of the subject—'hatha yoga'—involving physical posture exercises to achieve psychic power.

Most Western yoga practitioners do it merely as a form of healthful exercise, but Stephen Annett comments, 'It should be borne in mind that physical improvement in health is really incidental to the original aims of hatha yoga.' Its purpose is to prepare the mind for spiritual enlightenment, and most organizations teaching yoga include a degree of the basic Hindu philosophy underlying it as part of the course. How inextricably linked the two aspects are is open to debate. Some Indian Christians, for example, believe that yoga can be helpful to Christians; others suspect its Hindu roots and fear occult involvements.

The traditional medicine of Africa is still carried out today, alongside the orthodox medical work of hospitals and clinics. In Ghana, Kojo Goku makes a very successful living as a 'witch-doctor'. Here he is attempting to cure a paralysed man by rubbing him with a chicken, which he will then kill.

The ability to heal may be a function of the brain which is not normally released. At the age of two, Linda Martel underwent serious brain surgery. Miraculously she survived, and was then able to cure headaches, coughs and even paralysed limbs merely by touch.

IMPOSSIBLE FEATS

Stories of beds of nails or firewalking were once dismissed as mere travellers' tales. But not any more.

Many of the records in the *Guinness Book of Records* are constantly being challenged. But few people want to take on the two set by 'Komar' (Vernon Craig) of Wooster, Ohio. On 7 March 1975, Komar walked for 25 feet/7.5 m over blazing coals of elm wood at a measured temperature of 1183°F/640°C; and on 23 July four years earlier, he had completed 25 hours and 20 minutes on a bed of needle-sharp six-inch nails, spaced two inches apart from each other.

How did he do it? Dr Norman Shealy undertook numerous tests on him, and is reported to have found that Komar did *not* possess congenital analgesis (the medical condition which permits no physical awareness of pain). He was just as likely to suffer as anyone else. How are such feats possible?

Mayne Reid Coe, who trained himself to walk through fire and lick red-hot steel bars, believed that perspiration drops on the body might form a barrier between the heat and the performer's limbs. This may indeed be a factor, but it is certainly not enough to explain very long fire-walks, such as Komar's, nor to explain why the fire-walker's *clothing* does not catch fire either.

Harry Price, the noted psychic researcher, undertook some fire-walking experiments in 1935, and concluded that the secret lay in the fact that each foot touched the embers for less than half a second—not long enough to burn. But some Hindu fire-walks have been slow, dignified affairs; and again there is the question of the performer's clothing.

A spiritual power?

Probably the true explanation is that most fire-walkers go into a trance which induces anaesthesia. This would explain also the self-scarification rites carried out by the medium, or *dang-ki*, in the spiritist cults of Singapore. The *dang-ki* thrusts skewers through his cheeks and neck, and sits on a chair of sharp knives, to demonstrate the powers of his *shen* (possessing spirit) in protecting him from injury. It has been noticed that the *dang-ki*'s body becomes abnormally cold at the moment he is possessed by his *shen*.

Similar explanations may hold for the remarkable physical powers which can be produced by study of Eastern martial arts, which are closely bound up with spiritual exercises. The same applies to *tumo*, the Tibetan lama's art of body-heat projection, which protects him (despite his scanty clothing) against the rigours of Tibetan winters.

Stan Gooch believes that primitive peoples are better at these skills than Westerners because of 'a difference in the precise structure of the nervous system'. This may be so, but the phenomena can look very like demon possession too, and a degree of spirit influence should not be automatically discounted.

TODAY'S SUPER-POWERS

At least two present-day cults claim super-powers for their practitioners. TM (Transcendental Meditation), is a 'non-religious' meditation technique, which claims to increase people's personal vitality. Advanced students of TM can undergo the TM-Siddhi course, which promises skills such as levitation (the ability to rise a few feet from the ground while meditating), invisibility and clairvoyance.

Although pictures exist of meditators levitating, the movement is extremely reluctant to allow outsiders to witness it happening. Some observers theorize that the phenomenon may be more like a sudden hop in the air than a dignified floating

upwards, and so may be produced by involuntary jerks of the muscles, a frequent occurrence among meditators. Invisibility can be a mentally-induced phenomenon (if I *want* my hand to disappear, my brain may tell me eventually that it has done). On the other hand ex-meditation teacher R.D. Scott claims in his book *Transcendental Misconceptions* that demonic influence can be a factor in TM too.

Another group, Scientology, believes that its graduates— 'clears'—possess psychokinetic, clairvoyant and teleporting powers (see *Glossary*). Public demonstrations—now discontinued—have been remarkably unimpressive.

Is it possible to defy gravity? In the 'Indian rope trick', the magician, or *sadhu*, makes a pliable rope rise in the air and become rigid enough for a boy to climb up. It certainly looks genuine, though Western magicians perform similar feats merely by sophisticated trickery.

THE WAY TO ENLIGHTENMENT ?

There is plenty of evidence that our bodies and minds may possess powers which we have not yet learnt to use. And it is right that we should explore our potential to the full; but wrong to expect that by doing so we will necessarily find all the answers we are looking for or even find the personal fulfilment we desire.

According to the Bible, man is made in the image of God, and made good. But that image has

been ruined by the rebellion of human beings against their creator. Hence it is important to realize that exploring the nature of man will bring us face to face not only with our potential, but also with our fallen, sinful self. God is not 'within', the Bible teaches. Because of sin he is 'outside' our lives. Salvation must involve allowing him to restore both our relationship with himself and our true human nature.

At Kataragama in Sri Lanka, a fire-walking ceremony is held annually. Participants prepare themselves spiritually beforehand, and are completely unharmed by their slow barefoot walk over the red-hot embers.

MENTAL MYSTERIES

How does the mind work? As more studies are made, more complexity is found. And there are bizarre effects which seem to defy understanding.

Oliver Fox had always dreamed vividly—ever since his long spells of illness as a child. And in his teens, as an engineering student at Southampton, he discovered that he had a strange ability: to dream of a place, then pull himself physically into it until he felt a 'click' and arrived actually in the place he had dreamed about. In his 'dream body', that is; for his physical body was still lying in bed at home. He could walk around and observe his surroundings for a while, then—with another 'click'—reunite with his physical self.

Was this merely an illusion? He decided to put it to the test by projecting himself into an examination room the night before an exam, in order to look at the question paper. He memorized two questions; and both—one an extremely unusual question—came up in the 'real' paper next day.

Astral travel?
From experiences such as this, occult thinkers have derived the theory of 'astral projection'—the idea that each of us has a second body which can leave the sleeping physical body to take itself to other places as a fully conscious, thinking entity. In projection, emotions can be felt, intellectual decisions made, and sensory stimuli experienced. The 'astral body' rises out of the physical body through the head (Fox at first had headaches

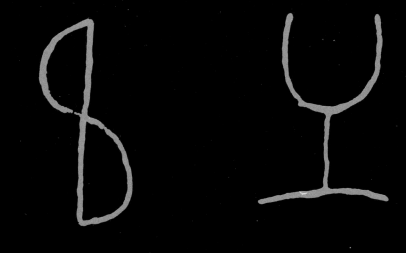

J. B. Rhine (right), with his most successful subject, Hubert Pearce. In card-guessing tests, Pearce consistently scored high above the statistical odds. Typically of ESP subjects, Pearce's extraordinary powers lasted for only a few years.

'A complete consecutive series of drawings transmitted by telepathy from Mr Guthrie to Miss E. without contact during the Liverpool experiment... When No. 6 was being transmitted, Miss E. said almost directly, "Are you thinking of the bottom of the sea, with shells and fishes?" and then, "Is it a snail or a fish?"—then drew as above.' (From the *Proceedings of the Society for Psychical Research, Volume II*).

J. B. RHINE

The study of the mind's extra-sensory perceptive abilities was first put on a scientific footing by Dr Joseph Banks Rhine, who coined such terms as 'ESP', 'parapsychology' and 'psi'. This pioneering North Carolina psychologist set standards of invincible integrity which are an example to all subsequent parapsychologists. In 1974, after 47 years of work, he realized that his right-hand man had been faking results, announced the fact publicly, and began immediately to develop a new method of analysis.

His initial work, between 1929 and 1934, seemed to afford staggering results, but as time passed and he tightened up his experimental controls the results proved more elusive.

'It is shocking but true,' he wrote, 'that we know the atom today better than we know the mind that knows the atom.'

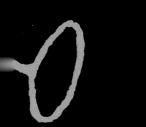

Originals

when projecting) and is connected to it by a 'silver cord' which lengthens as the second body moves away. At death, the cord breaks, and the bodies separate.

Astral projection has become the basis of a modern cult, Eckankar, but its 'reality' is impossible to prove. Remarkably convincing experiences can take place in dreams, and it is curious how many pioneers of astral travel had at one time or another suffered long periods of illness and been frustrated by the immobility of their physical bodies. It has been shown that drugs such as mescalin can produce very similar effects. Any information picked up (such as the examination questions) could arguably have

telepathic causes. At Stanford Research Institute in California some work has already been done on 'remote viewing'—the psychic ability to perceive scenes and events many miles away.

Many people have attempted to link the 'silver cord' of astral projection with a reference in the Bible's book of Ecclesiastes. However, the passage there refers merely to a cord suspending a golden oil-bowl from a ceiling. The theory of an astral body is foreign to the Bible. It is not to be identified with the 'soul', which Christians see as much more than just a bit of ghostly stuff floating within the body (see *Life after Life*).

Copies

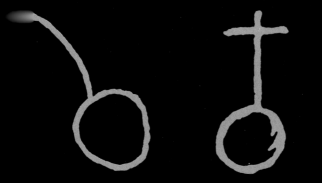

MINDFORCE

*Can the power of the mind bend a fork? Raise a table?
Produce what seem to be the effects of a ghost?*

Psychokinesis

One of the most controversial figures of the early
seventies was a young Israeli psychic named Uri
Geller. He shot to fame because of his ability to
bend forks and rings simply by stroking them; to
stop watches and clocks with the power of
thought; and to reproduce pictures which were
sealed inside an envelope. Was he an example of
remarkable psychokinesis ('PK' for short—see
Glossary), or simply a fraud? Conjuror James
Randi points out that Uri is an ex-night-club
illusionist who has been tested only by scientists,
never by professional fakers; and he offers to
reproduce all of Uri's 'paranormal' feats by
trickery alone.

Medical researcher Itzhak Bentov explains
Geller's feats as the activity of 'low-level
poltergeists', and certainly some of the
phenomena seem very similar. John White, one of
Uri's earliest scientific testers, now believes that
Uri has been duped and used by powers of evil in
the universe. Uri's former mentor, Andrija
Puharich, claimed that Uri was a channel for
communications from 'the Nine', mysterious
governors of this universe, and that he had been
contacted by space beings from Hoova, a planet
16,000 times the size of earth with an advanced
civilization whose life-span was a million years.

The extravagance of these claims has done
Geller's reputation no good, and recently he has
disavowed it. 'Concerning what Andrija believes
... that's totally up to him ... It could be a pure
energy force, a pure intelligence pattern. It could
be anything. It doesn't have to take the form of a
being.' Certainly the Hoovids' 'revelations'
through Uri have always been disappointingly
tame or bafflingly inscrutable. And it seems
unlikely that they would have singled out
someone like Uri, whose personal intelligence is
not great and whom Puharich admits is an
'unabashed egomaniac'.

A real force

But the powers of 'psychokinesis' which Geller
claims are not unique. A Russian housewife, Nina
Kulagina, has demonstrated the ability to move
small objects (matchsticks, pens and compass
needles) simply by concentrating her mind.
Felicia Parise and Ingo Swann in New York
possess similar powers. And whether or not Geller

**Uri Geller on television in
Denmark. As usual, his
broadcast affected clocks and
watches in viewers' homes.**

is a fraud, during his TV appearances clocks stop, forks bend and keys snap in the homes of viewers—clear evidence that *someone's* mind is exerting unusual energies.

The experiments of J.B. Rhine (see *Mental Mysteries*) suggest that our minds may be able to influence the fall of a dice, or the results of card guessing, much more than is usually assumed. Paranormal researchers now tend to regard ESP (see *Glossary*) and psychokinesis as dual aspects of one mysterious ability called 'psi'. Psi may well exist, as a spiritually neutral force. It remains to be shown that it could ever be harnessed for practical uses.

During seances (see *Contacting the Dead*), mediums often produce extraordinary physical effects. Here the medium Jack Webber is causing a table to levitate. Whether the power is coming from his mind or from some other source is not clear— nor is the cause of the marks at the bottom of this infra-red photograph.

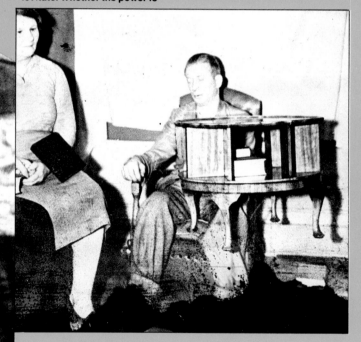

OBJECTS ON THE MOVE

Can an object suddenly dematerialize and reappear somewhere else? This is the claim of believers in 'apports'—which are articles (a button, a book, a loaf, a glass of wine, even a 39-inch snake or a four-foot-high plant) which suddenly appear in a room having apparently travelled instantaneously from another place.

Sometimes people appear to have been 'apported'; the Victorian medium Mrs Guppy, an extremely bulky lady, is said to have landed with a bump on the table in someone else's seance, holding an accounts book and a pen. Three theories are common.

● All reports are fraudulent. Apports rarely or never appear in test conditions, so this conclusion is just possible.

● There is a fourth dimension, a higher form of space into which objects can temporarily be lifted.

● A medium's mind can influence the molecular structure of objects. René Sudre has put forward this theory as an explanation of temporary dematerialization.

Any of these theories may be valid; there is certainly no need to invoke the spirit world for an answer.

When the great preacher John Wesley was a boy of 13, his home was invaded by 'Old Jeffrey'. This was the Wesley family's name for their pet 'ghost', who first manifested himself in strange knocking noises and dismal groans early in 1715. Soon other sounds were intermittently heard: footsteps on the stairs, the rustle of a gown, the sound of a rocking cradle. Family prayers were frequently interrupted by the noises.

The Wesleys grew accustomed to 'Old Jeffrey', and the youngest daughter, Kezzy, played a game of chasing 'him' from room to room. Then suddenly, two months after the first noises, 'Old Jeffrey' disappeared, and has never been back.

Was the Wesley family being haunted by some dead intelligence? Most ghost hunters would agree that it was not. 'Jeffrey' was a poltergeist; the German word means 'noisy spirit', and 'ghosts' of this type have produced a terrifying range of phenomena to disturb ordinary households—including messages written on walls, eerie voices, apports, physical blows, levitation, strange lights, furniture movements, disappearances of household items, even haircuts with invisible scissors.

Where does the power come from?

But few researchers today believe that spirits are responsible for producing poltergeists. There seem to be more obvious physical reasons. The Wesley episode, for example, was investigated by the scientist Joseph Priestley, and he observed that John's nineteen-year-old sister Hetty seemed to be the cause of the trouble. 'The disturbances were centred around Hetty's bed,' he reported, 'and were marked by Hetty's trembling in her sleep.'

Studies have shown that frequently in the house where a poltergeist manifests, there is a teenager passing through the sexual awakening of adolescence. It seems that the latent sexual energy is the cause of the trouble. Certainly poltergeists are all the more violent when sexual development is disturbed (as in the famous cases of Betsy Bell, who was probably molested by her father as a child, and Esther Cox, a victim of attempted rape), or when the person concerned has psychic abilities. Austrian medium Frieda Weisl possessed such violent sexual energies that objects would jump off the fireplace as she made love.

Power with a character

Despite their seemingly human origins, poltergeists appear to like attention. Phenomena will obligingly increase when encouraged—Kezzy Wesley was probably innocently responsible for multiplying 'Old Jeffrey's' efforts. In the Betsy

HOW DO THEY ACT?

Peter Underwood, President of the Ghost Club, makes four observations about poltergeists in his *Dictionary of the Supernatural*.

● Many of the adolescents involved are of above average intelligence, and usually in good health, though some are liable to hysterical bouts.

● Disturbances do not happen when the young person is sleeping normally, but when the unconscious brain is quite active. This suggests that the activity is connected with the higher centres of the brain.

● Objects transported through the air always travel downwards, from a higher level to a lower. This means that the minimum of energy is used.

● No one ever sees these objects *begin* to move, and often when someone observes an object in flight it falls to the ground straight away.

The most celebrated poltergeist case of recent years was in a house in Enfield in London. For years the house was disrupted by 'noisy ghosts', with heavy furniture overturned in the night. Unlike most poltergeist cases, the events were not related to one person. And since the house was also the scene of other paranormal events, it seems that more than just poltergeists were involved.

Bell case, an investigating committee of neighbours did more harm than good by encouraging the 'spirit' to perform certain tricks.

Failed attempts at exorcism, or seances held in houses dogged by poltergeists, can also result in stepped-up activity. But the sudden disappearance of the 'ghost' usually takes place as soon as the unknowing adolescent cause of the problem grows up a little bit more.

SEEING THE FUTURE

Tea leaves, yarrow sticks, animals' entrails. All these objects have been used in trying to find out what will happen tomorrow.

Did you read your horoscope this morning? Two-thirds of the British nation did—along with 53 per cent of the French, and 63 per cent of Germans. In America, 30,000 people each month buy a 'personalized' horoscope turned out by an IBM computer, but nonetheless there is plenty of work for 10,000 full-time and 175,000 part-time astrologers. Forecasting the future is a growth industry.

Astrology

Peter Sellers was one of many prominent people who has believed in astrology. 'The simple rules of astrology definitely work out in real life,' he insisted. 'I feel sure the planets must have some influence on our lives.' When the Beatles set up their recording company, Apple, they hired a professional astrologer to advise them. Even psychology professor Hans Eysenck has admitted that the stars may affect a person's choice of career.

Western astrology began when it was noticed that the sun seemed to move round the earth in a regular yearly path, spending about the same length of time in the vicinity of each of twelve groups of stars. These constellations of stars divided the heavens up into 'houses' (see diagram), and one's destiny was supposed to be dictated by which 'house' the sun was in—and which planets were in the same 'house'—when one was born. Serious astrologers insist on knowing the exact *moment* of birth before casting a horoscope; the date is not enough.

Many methods

Astrology is only one of many forms of forecasting which are gaining new popularity today. Recently the sophisticated woman's magazine *Cosmopolitan* produced a supplement explaining in detail to its 'liberated' readers how to read tea-leaves and coffee grounds, how to lay out tarot cards, and how to read palms.

Tarot cards contain pictures with various occult meanings, and when laid out in a certain order are claimed to spell out messages about the future. Closely similar is the ancient 'I Ching' method of throwing down yarrow sticks—or nowadays coins—and reading messages from the patterns formed.

Some of these forms of fortune-telling may merely be devices to enable people to tell themselves what they have already subconsciously decided. What one sees in a tea-cup, for example, or reads into the tarot message, will be shaped decisively by one's preoccupations and temperament. Gazing at a crystal ball ('scrying') is probably a form of automatism in

Once a partner in a firm of chartered surveyors, Ilyn Miller is now a high-society clairvoyant. She gives brandy-glass readings and 'tea and telepathy' afternoons as well as the more usual tarot readings. Ilyn sees her abilities as a gift which should be used to benefit other people.

ASTROLOGY

Astrology is completely unscientific.

● The planets are supposed to influence our lives—all except for Pluto and Neptune, which are ignored; they had not been discovered when astrological rules were formulated.

● A _thirteenth_ constellation, Ophiucus, is never mentioned.

● The sun does not spend an equal amount of time in each 'house'; its stays vary between six days in Scorpio and 47 in Virgo!

● The 'constellations' are not really natural groupings of stars; they only appear to be when viewed from earth. In fact, two stars in Orion are closer to earth than they are to one of their partners in the constellation!

● Most importantly, over the years the heavens have shifted. Thus despite the fact that astrologers still insist that someone born in early October is a Libra, a quick look at the sky shows that the sun is actually in Scorpio!

SCIENTIFIC FORTUNE-TELLING

In the 1960s the Rand Corporation of America developed a forecasting method called DELPHI in order to enable business firms to predict future trends accurately on the basis of advice by experts. Nothing occult was involved; DELPHI was a simple psychological tool.

But in 1979 a forecasting consultant named Francis Kinsman evolved a variant of the method, which he called TAROT, for gaining a picture of the world's future from the statements of astrologers, numerologists (see _Glossary_), clairvoyants, mediums and sensitives. As a result he published a report, _Future Tense_, which predicted world-wide economic collapse for 1982, a spate of earthquakes, a new Russian leader, and a Far East war in the late 1980s between Russia and China. Other events of the eighties were to be a 'bloodbath' in Africa, the collapse of the EEC, and the abdication of the Queen of England. TAROT represents a bizarre attempt to fuse a reliable method with uncommonly unreliable sources of data.

which the subconscious mind sends messages, in picture form, to the conscious self. And this explains the eagerness with which devotees tenaciously defend the reliability of their chosen method, often in the teeth of the evidence. But we do not know all the forces involved; it seems undeniable that a fascination with future-gazing can bring perilous spiritual consequences. ☞

SEEING THE FUTURE

Michel de Nostredame (1503–66) was already a well-known pioneering doctor when in 1555 he published his book *Centuries*. But within a few years this one cryptic book was to win him a massive, controversial reputation of a quite different kind.

'Nostradamus' was an astrologer, and *Centuries* contained a collection of inscrutable stanzas gathered in hundreds (hence 'centuries'), which purported to predict the future. Nostradamus' modern followers claim that he predicted accurately the Plague, the Great Fire of London, the French Revolution, Napoleon, the death of Pope John Paul I, and two World Wars.

In 1975, young British psychic Matthew Manning foresaw two disasters in dreams: the Boeing 747 crash at New York's Kennedy Airport and the Moorgate tube disaster in London. He suggested that 'great human anguish and pain ... generates energy that has the power to move backwards in time ... and can be "audible" before it occurs'.

JEANE DIXON

Jeane Dixon, an American society lady, has become perhaps the best-known 'prophet' of the twentieth century. She accurately predicted the assassinations of John F. Kennedy and Martin Luther King; and caused a sensation by predicting, on a visit to the Ambassador Hotel in Los Angeles, that Robert Kennedy would die violently in the same building. He did. However, she has made many mistakes. World War III did not begin in 1958, nor the Vietnam War end in 1966; Jackie Kennedy did remarry.

Mrs Dixon claims that her mistakes are caused by the fact that some 'revelations' can be turned aside if the person concerned knows what is predicted, while some are just 'telepathic vibrations'—strong signals of human intention, which can go wrong if the person concerned later changes his mind. This leaves her a wide margin for error. American researchers calculate that Mrs Dixon's 'score' of accurate prophecies has dropped sharply since 1970.

Nostradamus' accuracy is impossible to assess. His work is just too obscure, and some stanzas could refer either to trivial events of French court life or major international disasters. Certainly one quatrain refers to 'Hister'—Hitler?—a 'child of Germany'. But *both* sides in World War II were able to interpret Nostradamus as prophesying victory for them!

Premonitions

Sometimes ordinary people, too, have unusual precognition ('knowledge of future events'). Nine-year-old Eryl Mai Jones, for example, told her mother in October 1966 that she had dreamed of going to school and finding that 'something black had come down all over it'. Next day Eryl and 139 others died when half-a-million tons of coal waste slithered on to their Aberfan village school.

London psychiatrist Dr John Barker discovered 60 seemingly authentic premonitions of the Aberfan disaster. There were similar 'waves' of premonitions before the *Titanic* sinking and the

R-101 airship crash; so can impending doom be sensed? An American mathematician, William Cox, surveyed train crashes over several years and calculated that whenever a train crashed there were *invariably* fewer people on it than might have been expected. When a crash is coming, people change their bookings, decide not to travel, or choose an alternative route. The odds against his findings were over 100 to 1.

Lyall Watson explains this phenomenon as 'life's receptivity to very subtle stimuli that tell us that the future has already started'—on a par with the danger instinct in animals. Certainly animals show a high level of precognitive ability; in laboratory tests, mice were able to predict choices made by a random number generator, at odds of 1,000 to 1 against chance.

Laboratory tests on humans, however, have been largely disappointing. Whether or not precognition exists, it seems it cannot be controlled at will.

San Francisco in California, USA, has suffered many violent earthquakes. In 1906, 700 people died and 250,000 were made homeless. Today, the city has two 'premonitions bureaux' so that members of the public can report their premonitions of future disasters.

WHAT DO WE WANT TO KNOW?

It is not difficult to see *why* people want to know the future. In an uncertain world, where the rate of change is constantly speeding up and 'future shock' is forever exposing us to unpleasant surprises, it gives us a sense of power and security to feel that we are forewarned.

But exactly *which facts* do we need to know for our own good? 'Unless man were to be like God and know everything,' wrote John Buchan, 'it is better that he should know nothing.' The Bible's attitude is quite clear. Partial revelations of future events may be quite useless and irrelevant; but the Creator himself is prepared to guide us directly if we depend on him.

JINXES AND CURSES

When five people have all had accidents in the same car, can it be coincidence?

At 19,000 tons, the *Great Eastern* was the largest ship in the world. But it seemed also to be the most deadly. While it was being built, a riveter and his boy apprentice mysteriously disappeared. When it was ready for launching, it became stuck in the slipway and took three months to free. After the launching, its builder collapsed on deck with a stroke. He was dead within a week.

But this was just a start. One of the funnels exploded; five firemen died, and another was crushed by the paddle wheel; the captain drowned; a man was lost overboard; the paddle wheel claimed another victim. The ship's mounting catalogue of disasters gave her such a bad reputation that she started losing money heavily, and only 15 years after launching was abandoned to rust at Milford Haven.

Coincidence or reality?

Are there such things as 'jinxes' or 'curses' which hang around certain objects or people, luring them to destruction? There are thousands of stories supplying evidence, but we must remember that two or three cases of misfortune can seem like an incredible sequence to the people concerned, yet actually be mere coincidence. Also, once an object is thought of as evil, all kinds of other 'evidence' will suddenly accumulate—much of it circumstantial or wishful thinking.

Yet some cases are well-documented, suggesting that not all curse stories are tall tales. The Lockheed Constellation aircraft AHEM-4 caused four years of disasters before crashing with no survivors in 1949. The car in which Archduke Ferdinand was assassinated had seven subsequent owners who suffered serious (usually fatal) accidents. The Porsche in which James Dean died in 1955 was similarly ill-fated.

Sometimes distinguished families claim their own ancestral curses. The Bowes-Lyons, Earls of Strathmore, inherit the 'Horror' of Glamis. No one outside the family knows what the affliction is, but the heir of Strathmore is told the secret by his father, tradition has it, on his twenty-first birthday. Females are not told. A former Lord Strathmore remarked to a friend, 'If you could know of it, you would thank God you were not me.'

The Alexandra Palace in London was destroyed by fire in 1980. There have been many theories about the cause of the fire—this group of psychical researchers believed that leys were to blame (see *The Unknown Earth*). But local inhabitants recall that an old gypsy laid a curse on the palace at the time it was built.

Warnings of disaster

In Ireland, the banshee, or *bansidhe* (from the Gaelic word for 'fairy woman') is a weird spirit creature whose blood-chilling wail is supposed to presage a human death. Banshees are really guardian spirits rather than harbingers of doom, but their cry always spells disaster. The banshee wailed for ancient Irish heroes, such as Brian Boru and Finn MacCool, but was also reported in County Cork in 1922 when Irish revolutionary fighter Michael Collins died in an ambush, and in 1963 when the Irish-American President John F. Kennedy was assassinated.

Other nations have similar traditions, and some accounts are fairly convincing. Sheila St Clair suggests that the banshee is 'part of an inherited memory . . . stamped on our racial consciousness' suddenly released by the mind 'as a kind of subliminal "four-minute warning" so that we may prepare ourselves for that tragedy'.

HOW DO CURSES WORK?

Extra-sensory forces
Traditionally, curses can be placed on other people by methods such as spells, sticking pins into wax images and reciting incantations. Possibly the intense concentration involved can bring some psychic power to bear on the victim's mind.

The power of suggestion Often in a primitive tribe, a man who knows he has been cursed will simply lie down and die—not necessarily because of the curse, but because he is convinced that he will die anyway.

'Psychic tape-recording' Peter Underwood believes that 'somehow, thought or feeling can imprint itself on an object or person in such a way as to be picked up by other people; if the thought is malevolent, then the effect can be unpleasant.'

Supernatural activity Colin Wilson has shown that some stories of cursings suggest active malice by a real, personal disincarnate entity. Christians would recognize this as an 'evil spirit'. Certainly the power of curses is unpredictable and dangerous; those who try to capture it usually find that it has captured them. Christians believe that the powers of evil have been conquered by Christ's death, and that this victory over evil can be exercised by Christians today.

The cult of voodoo thrives in the Caribbean. Images such as this doll are used both to attract the power of spirits and to focus evil power on other people as a curse.

WICCA AND MAGICK

Witches have never had it so good.
Today, their craft is legal – and profitable.

The occultist Aleister Crowley attracted many followers. Here he is seen performing a ceremony in one of his occult groups. In 1920 he founded a secret society in Sicily, but within two years he had been expelled by the other members.

This elaborate ceremony on a snow-covered moor may be nothing more than a publicity exercise. But it is certain that witches' covens meet regularly throughout the world thirteen times a year.

Today in London an ex-priest and psychic called Alex Sanders is openly involved in initiating new witches and supervising several covens. Sybil Leek, perhaps the first millionairess witch in the world, has made a fortune from books, television appearances and syndicated articles.

This marks quite a change in the public attitude to witches. Between the fifteenth and eighteenth centuries in Western Europe, it was serious business. While a few 'witch finders', such as the notorious Matthew Hopkins, grew rich from detecting it, thousands of others—many of them undoubtedly innocent—died by fire or water.

Why witchcraft?

Who were the witches? Their opponents said they were in league with the devil; there seems little evidence of that. Historians now believe that the witchcraft 'craze' had its origins in the medieval church's fascination with demons; being a witch, or fantasizing about being one, was a secret way of thumbing one's nose at the 'establishment', which included a very wealthy and powerful church. Keith Thomas, in his book *Religion and the Decline of Magic*, suggests that it offered 'a way of bettering one's condition when all else had failed ... a substitute for impotence, a remedy for anxiety and despair'.

Earlier this century, however, one distinguished scholar, Margaret Murray, claimed that witchcraft in Europe had been a systematic religion, the true 'Old Religion' which had always

SATANISM

Since Anton LaVey began his First Church of Satan in 1966, several organizations have sprung up around the world dedicated to the worship of Satan. They generally do not think of Satan so much as a personal figure (which is the way he is presented in the Bible), but as an abstract principle of evil, 'a dark, hidden force that was responsible for the workings of earthly affairs for which science and religion had no explanation and no control'.

Satanic weddings and funerals are held, but so, too, are lust rituals and destruction rituals. One researcher, Burton Wolfe, comments, 'Satanism is a blatantly selfish, brutal religion. It is based on the belief that man is inherently a selfish, violent creature, that life is a Darwinian struggle for survival of the fittest...'

Satanists are relatively open about their activities, by contrast with the other main group who worship Satan—devotees of black magic. The main ceremony of black magic is the Black Mass, a ceremony of worship of the devil which is an obscene parody of the Roman Catholic rite; occasionally in history it has been attended by human sacrifice and perhaps even cannibalism. Satan is worshipped as a power-conferring alternative deity to the God of the Bible.

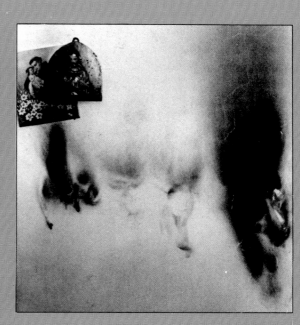

It seems clear that individuals can be affected by evil spirits. The process of casting out an evil spirit, exorcism, is recognized by the medical profession. In a dramatic exorcism in Rome in 1972, flames appeared in the room, leaving these marks on the wall. The power of exorcism lies not in some formula of words, but in the power of the God who answers prayer.

WICCA

'Wicca' beliefs are much closer to Eastern religions than to Christianity. Witches believe in a Supreme Being who, says Hans Holzer, is not a person but merely 'a great principle, a spiritual force'. Sybil Leek explains, 'From this Supreme Being comes life, and by a process of many incarnations, ascending a spiral of spiritual development, we are drawn back into the life force.' The Supreme Being is worshipped in the figure of a Mother Goddess, and sometimes also a male horned god.

The witch Madge Worthington predicts that wicca 'will supersede Christianity—certainly by the end of the century, if not before'. There are no signs that this is happening.

MAGICK

Not all magic is worked by witches. Today's 'magick' (the spelling often used to distinguish it from conjuring tricks) derives from the secret practices of early twentieth-century occult groups, such as the Order of the Golden Dawn, and figures such as Aleister Crowley, self-styled 'wickedest man in the world'.

A large occult body in America, the Rosicrucians (split into two main rival groups) perpetuates magick teachings. It claims to be non-religious, but its teachings involve assumptions about the nature of the universe which conflict with Christianity. Modern magick groups derive their views from ancient traditions of the cabbala and alchemy.

Magick has existed in every age, and requires two anti-Christian assumptions: first, that certain objects or activities contain inherent spiritual power; second, that we can and should employ this power to affect others.

existed secretly as an alternative to Christianity. Although now discredited, her views were widely accepted for a long time. She even wrote the article on witchcraft for the 1929 *Encyclopaedia Britannica*. Eventually Gerald Gardner, a student of the occult, began to found covens of witches to 'revive' the 'Old Religion'. His attempts bore fruit; today covens exist throughout the world. The name his followers give to their faith is 'wicca'.

What is it like?

Witches distinguish between *black magic*, which involves devil worship and the practice of evil; and *white magic*, which is used for good purposes. But even white magic involves claiming for oneself godlike powers over other human lives, and it can be used with a chilling lack of morality. Explaining some dubious deeds of her own, Sybil Leek claims that 'evil may be justified if it is for the greater good of the whole'.

In view of this, it is not surprising that the Bible opposes witchcraft of any kind. Present-day 'wicca' is founded insecurely on Murray's exploded historical research, hazardous moral practices, and promises of limited spiritual powers which are a pale shadow of the power of the living God.

PYRAMIDS

Only one of the seven wonders of the world survives – the pyramids of ancient Egypt. And their mystery is as fascinating today as ever.

No-one would dispute that the Great Pyramid of Cheops is one of the wonders of the world. The 90 million cubic feet of stone in it (covering an area of about 14 acres/5.6 hectares) would build 30 Empire State Buildings, or all the churches, chapels and cathedrals in England. The two and a half million blocks of limestone are fitted together so tightly that the gaps between them are minute. The sides are aligned exactly to face north, south, east and west. But what is the whole thing for?

A fortress tomb?

Most modern Egyptologists believe that it was simply a fortress-tomb for the Pharaoh Khufu, or Cheops. They point out that this seems to have been the purpose of each of the 40 major pyramids built along the Nile, and that the Great Pyramid contains an imposing sarcophagus, obviously built into the pyramid as an integral feature (the doors are too narrow for it to be moved in or out). Unfortunately, nobody has ever found any bodies in any of the pyramids!

Were the bodies removed by grave robbers? Possible, but unlikely; grave robbers usually stole the rich burial trappings and left the bodies behind. Did the priests remove the bodies to foil robbers? That seems more likely. Or are the bodies still there, but in as yet undiscovered secret chambers? If so, the sarcophagi so far discovered would simply be decoys.

The Great Pyramid of Cheops, at Giza in Egypt.

A store of knowledge?

Another possibility, suggested by the careful mathematical construction of the Great Pyramid is that the primary purpose of the whole building project was to embody certain geometric, astronomical and occult data. It has been claimed that the Pyramid reveals the precise circumference of the earth, the mean length of the earth's orbit around the sun, the specific density of the earth, the speed of light, and the weight of this planet.

It is hard to tell how much of this is wishful thinking. Using the same processes, one could extract exactly the same figure for the earth's density from the Eiffel Tower! And since about 33 ft/10 m are missing from the top of the pyramid, we can only guess about its exact dimensions and weight. It is claimed that the perimeter of the pyramid indicates the length of the solar year, when measured in special 'pyramid inches'; but if so, the pyramid builders must have believed that each year contained 362.76 days!

Last century 'pyramidologists' claimed to read predictions about the future in the dimensions of the pyramid. Since this involved the Second Coming of Christ in 1881, 1936 or 1953 (depending on one's interpretation), and the completion of God's final judgement for 20 August 1953, 'pyramidiocy' is now firmly discredited.

PYRAMID POWER

In the early 1930s Antoine Bovis was on holiday in Egypt when he became fascinated to find that small animals which had wandered into the pyramids and died had not decomposed. Their bodies had been perfectly mummified. After experiments he came to believe that fruit and vegetables could be kept fresh longer under a cardboard model of a pyramid. He was ridiculed, but some years later a Czech radio technician named Karl Drbal patented a pyramid-shaped object which he declared would sharpen razor blades. It is now claimed by believers that pyramids can improve the taste of food, enhance plant growth, aid meditation, assist restful sleep, induce clairvoyance, and even halt ageing.

Experiments with a Gauss meter suggest that the pyramid shape may indeed induce magnetism, and the force field created may in some circumstances provoke electromagnetic dehydration. But since similar magnetic fields do not produce similar results, other energies may be at work. It remains to be seen whether this is a genuine scientific discovery or an occult curiosity.

ANCIENT ENGINEERING

'All that can be learn'd from them,' said Daniel Defoe, 'is that there they are.'

For centuries there has been no explanation for the scores of standing stones which form gaunt circles all over the British Isles. Some of them (especially Avebury, in Wiltshire, and Stonehenge) are clearly major ancient monuments.

Who built them, and why?

Recent research at Stonehenge demonstrates that its builders knew a great deal about astronomy and geometry. 'A veritable Newton or Einstein must have been at work,' comments astronomer Sir Fred Hoyle. Without any system of writing, the builders were able to construct, teach and retain a knowledge of mathematics scarcely inferior to Egyptian knowledge of the same

period. And even today we have no good idea how the major stones were erected into place.

Facts such as these have tempted people such as the writer Tom Lethbridge, and less intelligently Erich von Däniken, to speculate that the construction may have owed something to ancient astronaut visitors. Lethbridge theorized that the stones might have been giant markers for the guidance of aircraft or spaceships. There is no evidence for this view, and much against it: the site clearly had other functions; it is hard to see what use the markers in their present locations could have been to aircraft; and there are strong arguments against contacts with alien spacemen (see *Close Encounters*).

Cosmic proportions

John Michell claims that Stonehenge was based on the same set of 'cosmic proportions' as Glastonbury Abbey, Chartres Cathedral, the Pyramids, and Solomon's Temple. These figures, he says, derive from the data given about the New

Jerusalem in the Book of Revelation, but to find them one must read the Bible 'properly'—in other words, in terms of the secret, occult wisdom of Gnostic gematria (see *Glossary*), the mysticism of the early Christians.

Michell's theory is so much romantic moonshine. For one thing, the Gnostics were not early Christian leaders, but interloping heretics, rejected vigorously as sub-Christian by Jesus' first followers. Revelation is not a Gnostic book. Furthermore, Michell's calculations do not add up. He has to assume that the builders of Stonehenge thought in terms of two different measuring systems—cubits and feet—simultaneously; he changes some of the actual data in Revelation to 'commensurable proportions' to make it fit. Finally, he has to *guess* one of the most critical figures on which the entire calculation depends.

Colin Wilson says that Stonehenge and other sites were 'apparently intended to be giant accumulators of magic power'. There may be indications of this in the associations with leys and underground streams (see *Tapping Natural Forces*). But all we can say with confidence is that the sites were used both for ritual purposes and as astronomical observatories. Which may be all that there is to know.

GLASTONBURY

The town of Glastonbury is situated on leys which also pass through Avebury and Stonehenge, and strange legends have long been associated with it. From 1191, it has been proclaimed the burial place of the mystical British king Arthur and his wife Guinevere. A strong local tradition asserts that Joseph of Arimathea came to Glastonbury after Christ's crucifixion and built the first church there.

In 1964 an occultist named Mrs Maltwood announced that she had discovered Glastonbury Tor to be surrounded by a 'temple of the stars', a zodiac formed out of natural features such as fields, banks, rivers and earthworks. Earlier this century, the 'Glastonbury Scripts'—examples of automatic writing (see *Glossary*) obtained by the Abbey's Director of Excavations, Frederick Bligh Bond—claimed that secret gnostic techniques had been used in the construction of the Abbey. All of this points to some strong local occult connections, although the specific legends may be unfounded.

At midsummer every year, ceremonies are still held at Stonehenge, England, by people who believe that the site has religious significance.

REINCARNATION

Hindus and Buddhists believe that after death, the soul moves to a new body. Today an increasing number of people in the West share this belief.

In 1935, the Deva family in India grew worried about the strange behaviour of their daughter Shanti. She had begun to talk incessantly about a place called Muttra where, she said, she had lived in a previous life. Her name had been Ludgi. She had been the mother of three children, and had died in giving birth to the third.

Her stories were dismissed as fanciful knowledge—until by accident they discovered that a woman called Ludgi had died in precisely those circumstances at Muttra. Taken to Muttra, Shanti lapsed into the local dialect without ever having learned it; recognized her 'husband' and the two older children; and described her former home before she had seen it.

A world-wide belief

Stories such as this are often claimed to prove reincarnation, the idea that after death human beings are born again as babies to live another life. Reincarnation features in several world religions (Hinduism, Buddhism, Sikhism, Jainism, some Islamic sects and Christian heresies) as well as present-day cults such as Scientology and Theosophy. Opinion polls show a steady rise in the number of people accepting the belief.

Two of the main sources of evidence for the idea are *déjà vu* experiences and 'hypnotic regression'. *Déjà vu* is what happens when a person has the curious feeling that he has visited a certain place before, or has witnessed a certain event before.

LIFE AND DEATH

What does the Bible say about life after death?

● There will be a day of judgement when all the dead will stand before God. They will be judged according to whether or not they believed in Jesus Christ. Those who trusted him to forgive their sins will enter God's kingdom. Unbelievers will go into eternal punishment.

● Jesus claimed that his life, death and resurrection brought a totally new world order. When it is completed, believers will be given a new body—as Jesus was at his resurrection—and take part in the new creation. So Christians believe not only in the survival of the spirit, but also in the resurrection of the body.

● The Old Testament describes the state of death as being darkness, silence, rest, and the absence of thought and memory. No one comes back from the grave, but death does not end existence and God is able to bring men out of the grave.

● The New Testament continues this picture. The dead are asleep, but there is a difference between those who died believing in Jesus, and those who rejected him. Believers are 'with Christ'; the others are 'spirits in prison'.

In 1966, Dr Hemendra Banerjee flew to England from India to investigate the case of the Pollock twins. Had they lived before? Their father believed that they were reincarnations of his previous two daughters, killed in a car crash nine years earlier.

Though it has been suggested that this is the memory of a previous existence there is much evidence to suggest that *déjà vu* is simply a minor brain malfunction. It tends to occur more readily under conditions of fatigue, or in some types of epilepsy. Many doctors think it can be explained as an unsynchronized electrical discharge in a part of the brain associated with memory functions. The phenomenon has sometimes been evoked by electrical stimulation of the brain under surgery.

Returning to previous lives

'Hypnotic regression' stems from the famous case of 'Bridie Murphy' in 1954, in which a young American housewife was hypnotized and began talking as if she were living in nineteenth-century Ireland. Since then 'hypnotherapists' such as Arnall Bloxham have 'regressed' many patients to past lives, and have tape-recorded the results. Although it is often unaccountably difficult to check out the specific details given by the 'regression', many of the stories told have been remarkably accurate and perfectly plausible.

The 'Wheel of Life' represents the Hindu idea of reincarnation. Hindus believe that we are trapped in an endless cycle of lives, fated to experience rebirth after rebirth until we become pure enough to stop returning. At this stage we lose all personal identity and merge with the impersonal Infinite, Brahman.

WHAT IS REGRESSION?

The difficulty with the question of reincarnation is that all the evidence is completely unverifiable. And it can all be read in several different ways.

Tricks of the mind? Some cases of 'hypnotic regression' have proved to be merely 'cryptomnesia'. The mind plays a trick on itself, imagining and describing in detail a fantasy life.

Unconscious memory? We know that the brain can retain information which we have not consciously stored. Could some regression accounts be the release of such information?

Telepathy? We do not know exactly how the brain picks up information. Is the subject of regression picking up information telepathically from the brains of others—perhaps even from some who have died?

Race memory? Some have suggested that there is such a thing as 'race memory' which is inherited from ancestors and released under special conditions. It has also been suggested that walls and rooms can store information traces.

Effects of hypnotism? We do not know just what hypnotism is. For years it was thought to be a kind of sleep; that theory has now been proved wrong. So we cannot know the full effects of hypnotism on our consciousness.

Nor is this all. If I have lived through several lifetimes, which of those personalities is the real me? If the answer is, 'None of them, but a type of ''super-self'' that presides over them all,' then why am I never conscious of that super-self's existence? How can I prove that it is real?

LIFE AFTER LIFE?

A serious accident. A patient recovers from the critical list. He claims to have seen a future life. Is this fact or fantasy?

Thomas Welch was an engineer's helper for a lumber company in Oregon. One day he was walking along a narrow trestle, suspended 55 ft/ 16 m above a dam, when he slipped and fell into water ten feet deep. His body was not found for almost an hour; and when he was revived, he claimed to have been to hell.

'It's easy to talk about and describe something you have seen,' he stated. 'I know there is a lake of fire because I have seen it. I know Jesus Christ is alive in eternity. I have seen him.'

Out-of-the-body experiences

What had happened? Welch had experienced an 'OBE' ('out-of-the-body experience'). The same thing commonly happens to patients undergoing critical surgery who 'die' for a few minutes on the operating table. When revived, they often claim to have had glimpses of an after-life. Usually they find their experience difficult to communicate in words, but they are never as frightened of dying again.

In the late 1970s a group of doctors arose who styled themselves 'thanatologists'—students of what happens at death. Dr Raymond Moody's book *Life after Life*, detailing hundreds of OBEs, became an international best-seller. Moody, a Methodist, claims that none of his research proves or disproves the existence of a final judgement, hell or heaven (although some resuscitees report a 'city of light' which sounds like heaven); but other writers are less cautious.

Dr Maurice Rawlings, for instance, claims that OBEs prove the truth of Christianity. Unfortunately, some resuscitees testify that the spirit beings tell them otherwise; Rawlings dismisses these experiences as demonic counterfeits. But how can he judge which experiences are true and which false? Some OBEs include meetings with Krishna and other pagan figures; Rawlings assumes the resuscitees have really met Jesus and wrongly identified him. But this seems an unwarranted assumption.

In fact, thanatological experiences 'prove' very little. They afford ground for fascinating speculation, but no more.

OUT-OF-THE-BODY EXPERIENCES

This composite account of what happens after death was compiled by Raymond Moody from the experiences of several resuscitees.

● You are dying. As the pain reaches its climax, you hear the doctor pronounce you dead.

● An uncomfortable buzzing or ringing noise begins, and you feel yourself moving quickly down a long dark tunnel.

● As you emerge, you realize that you are still in the same place—but *outside* your body. You watch as medical staff try to resuscitate the body you once lived in.

● Others appear to help you— including spirits of friends and relatives, and a 'being of light' who projects love and warmth.

● The being of light asks a question to make you assess the worth of your life, and simultaneously you experience an 'instant replay' of your life's major experiences.

● You find yourself approaching a sort of barrier, seemingly the border between earthly life and the next world, but realize you must return; your life is not yet over.

● You resist, but somehow are returned to your earthly body and regain consciousness. . .

WHAT DOES IT PROVE?

The evidence for thanatology rests on very flimsy grounds. Many of the leading writers are doctors, but most have no medical experience of the cases which they relate.

● Not all OBEs tell the same story; many are contradictory, and Moody's 'pattern' experience (outlined above) is a compilation from different people's accounts—no one person experienced every detail listed.

● What happens in OBEs is impossible to determine. Is the body really 'dead'? There are currently three competing definitions of clinical death; it is hard to tell the exact moment at which someone passes from life to death.

● Is the OBE a real experience, or merely a fantasy conjured up by some region of the patient's brain? There is no way of telling. But it is suspicious that what dying people claim to see often fits their own personal theological beliefs (or fears).

Out-of-the-body experiences, for example after serious accidents, are the source of most of the ideas on 'thanatology', the study of what happens at death. The world's leading thanatologist is

Dr Elisabeth Kubler-Ross. However, her reputation has been somewhat tarnished since it was revealed that she received much of her information from 'spirit guides' at seances.

MEN WHO NEVER DIED

The wandering Jew... The flying Dutchman... History is full of legends of men condemned to live for ever.

In 1228 an Armenian archbishop, visiting London, mentioned that in his country there was a man named Cartaphilus who claimed to have been Pontius Pilate's doorkeeper. As Jesus had staggered past bearing his cross, Cartaphilus had struck him and jeered; at which Christ commented, 'I go, and you will wait till I return.' He had then been incapable of death, doomed to wander the world for ever until Christ's return at the end of time.

When last heard of, Cartaphilus was apparently baptized and living among monks, devoutly hoping for salvation. Perhaps, though, his hopes were disappointed, for in 1542 he introduced himself to Paulus von Eitzen, Lutheran bishop of Schleswig, this time under the name Ahasuerus. A pamphlet bearing the story circulated throughout Europe—its popularity perhaps explained by the anti-Semitism of the period—and sightings of the 'Wandering Jew' were reported widely. His last known port of call was Salt Lake City in 1868.

The story of the Wandering Jew merely reflects the human fascination with the medieval idea of endless life. Although the story has been a stimulus for poetry, art and drama, there is no shred of evidence for its truth. Apart from anything else, since Christ was prepared to forgive his killers as he hung on the cross, it seems monstrously out of character for him to condemn one man eternally for a single blow. The Christ of the legend is more like a testy wizard than the real Jesus.

Count St Germain

A less straightforward, modern version of the legend concerns the mysterious eighteenth-century occultist, Count St Germain, who moved in the highest courtly circles and counted Cagliostro and Mesmer among his occult apprentices. He claimed to be able to transmute base metals into gold, to enlarge and improve diamonds, and to perform astral travel. Less exotically, he was a superb linguist, pianist, inventor and raconteur.

We first hear of him in 1710, when he looked as if he was in his forties—and last in 1820, which would make him at least 150 years old. This may not be true, but he was certainly active for over 90 years, and there are well-witnessed reports of

Reports of Ahasuerus, the Wandering Jew, were circulated widely through Europe in the seventeenth century.

meetings with him after his supposed burial in 1784. Consequently, many occultists believe he never died, and that he still appears sporadically today. More than one mystical group claims to be led directly by him, and occasional claimants come forward professing to be St Germain.

The story is undoubtedly strange, but there is no real evidence that St Germain still lives.

VAMPIRES

Ever since Bram Stoker wrote the novel *Dracula* in 1897, legends about vampires have been well known. The popular ideas include the following elements:

● Vampires are unquiet spirits who leave their tombs nightly to suck the blood of the living.

● Vampires look like other men, but cast no shadow and cause no reflection in mirrors.

● The vampire's spirit can be laid to rest by driving a stake through the exhumed body.

● Garlic and crosses are protection against vampire attack.

These ideas about 'the undead' derive from Slavic superstitions. Slav religion was based on manism (ancestor worship) and bodies were ritually exhumed for various purposes. It came to be believed that those who had died suddenly—unmarried brides-to-be, for instance—were still greedy for the joys of life, and would return to imperil the living. The vampire legends developed from there, and between 1700 and 1740 there was an epidemic of vampire 'attacks' right across Europe. Colin Wilson speculates, 'It could be that vast numbers of people . . . began to brood on the reports of vampires . . . Huge quantities of psychic energy suddenly became available to the flotsam and jetsam of the spirit world.'

In 1785, at the age of 115, Count St Germain (left) still looked in the prime of life. The elaborate reception has been laid on by him for Cagliostro, another occult follower. Today there are still claims that St Germain is alive—now aged over 300.

GHOSTS AND APPARITIONS

Gothic horror stories are guaranteed to make the flesh creep.
But is there truth behind the fiction?

Mrs Pacquet felt strangely depressed. The mood had been upon her since her awakening that dull Chicago morning, and there seemed no real reason. Then, just as she turned from reaching for some tea from the pantry, suddenly she saw her brother Edmund standing a few feet away. He was falling forward with a rope around his legs. 'The vision lasted but a moment ... but was very distinct. I dropped the tea, clasped my hands to my face, and exclaimed, "My God! Ed is drowned."' Ed had been—only six hours before.

A telepathic message?
It is common for bereaved people to imagine vividly that they have seen the deceased, but Mrs Pacquet's experience was much more than this. However, it was far from unusual. Apparitions like this often appear when the person concerned is undergoing some form of crisis—illness, accident or death. The Society for Psychical Research, who put together a *Census of Hallucinations* in 1889, concluded that such apparitions were unconscious telepathic messages from the crisis victim to his friend or relative.

This seems quite plausible—we know very little about how the mind perceives objects; hypnosis or dreams can change our perceptions remarkably—but probably the 'receiver' mind has more to do with constructing the apparition than the 'sender'. This is because usually (unlike Mrs Pacquet's brother) the apparition looks quite well and normal, giving no clue of the crisis being undergone; and it seems quite solid and three-dimensional, casting a shadow, causing reflections in mirrors, adapting itself completely to its physical surroundings.

What about 'collective' apparitions, seen by more than one person? The SPR had collected no less than 130 of these by 1943. Do these prove that a dead person has actually manifested himself to the living? Not necessarily; there have also been 'collective apparitions' of people who were existing happily somewhere else at the moment when their apparition was seen. It seems more likely that in collective cases one of the viewers is responsible for receiving the apparition telepathically from its source, and that he unconsciously transfers the visual information to the others there with him.

An apparition of someone unknown to the viewer is more difficult to explain. But perhaps in some situations at some times our minds are unusually receptive to messages. Or perhaps someone else we know, who *did* know the source of the apparition, has transmitted the necessary information to our minds.

Most alleged pictures of ghosts are rather dubious. But experts who have examined these photographs, taken in Winchester Cathedral, England, say that there is no question of their being fakes. Both pictures show the altar, but when the second one was developed, a group of figures in medieval robes was visible. Witnesses say there was nobody in front of the camera when the picture was taken.

HAUNTINGS

Apparitions are one type of ghost. Hauntings are quite different. Apparitions usually happen only once, look solid, and communicate quite naturally; hauntings are usually repetitive, may look quite unconnected with the surroundings, and pay no attention to onlookers. Over a period of time, haunting ghosts may become fainter and fainter, like a battery running down.

Philosopher H.H. Price suggested that there might be a 'psychic ether' on which mental imprints could be made; thus a haunting would be a playback of a 'recording' made on the ether. Since observing a haunting is often quite like watching a silent film, this suggestion seems plausible.

LIFE AFTER DEATH

There are many possible explanations of apparitions. They certainly show that our visual ability is more complicated than we usually imagine, and is closely linked with our subconscious. But they cannot be taken as evidence to support the idea of life after death.

It is interesting in this context to look at the resurrection of Jesus. The Bible states that on the Sunday after his crucifixion, his dead body had disappeared from its sealed tomb. A handful of his followers saw Jesus alive that day, and over the next six weeks many hundreds of other people did so, too. But the Bible makes it clear that the risen Jesus was not an apparition. Indeed, he went to some lengths to prove this, by encouraging people to touch him, and by eating food. To his followers, now as then, his physical resurrection was proof that through his death, Jesus had made available a new quality of life which would not end with physical death.

CONTACTING THE DEAD

The pianist John Lill claims to be in contact with Beethoven. Mediums claim to receive messages for the bereaved. Can the living really contact the dead?

This strange conversation was carried out at Borley Rectory, known for a century as the most haunted house in England. As well as apparitions and phantom noises, messages would appear written on the walls. The activity was most intense when Lionel Foyster was rector—his wife Marianne seems to have attracted many of the events (see *Mindforce*).

José Nunes and his friend Mauricio were playing with a gun one day when it went off. The ricocheting bullet killed Mauricio. Although José immediately called the police, he was arrested for murder.

His mother contacted Brazil's top medium, Francisco Xavier, who claims that the dead occasionally control his hand and write messages. He produced a piece of automatic writing which read, 'José was not to blame . . . I was killed as a result of a foolish game.' Impressed, the judge freed José. The writing matched Mauricio's handwriting exactly.

Talking with the dead

Was Mauricio communicating from beyond the grave? Ever since the Fox sisters there have been innumerable attempts to extract messages from the dead, including automatic writing, table rapping, spirit tapes and photographs, and the ouija board or planchette. Mediums in entranced states have produced not only astoundingly correct information (although usually of an utterly trivial nature) but also sometimes 'ectoplasm' (supposedly the substance of which spirits are composed). This material issues from their bodies, sometimes taking shape as a hand or

When in a trance, some mediums apparently exude a substance called ectoplasm which can materialize into recognizable shapes. In 1921 in Warsaw, Franek Kluski materialized a pair of hands, and was able to take this wax impression of them before they dematerialized.

THE LIFE BEYOND?

The Bible's teaching about life after death conflicts profoundly with the information about 'the other side' usually offered by spirits. Witness the report given by a spirit who was allegedly the son of Bishop James Pike.

Pike
'I haven't heard anything personally about Jesus. Nobody around me seems to talk about him. When we come over here, we have a choice, to remain as we are, or to grow in our understanding. Some still seem to be church minded and are waiting for a Judgement Day, but these seem to be the unenlightened ones.'

The Bible
'(In heaven) there shall no more be anything accursed, but the throne of God and of the Lamb (Jesus) shall be in it, and his servants shall worship him; and they shall see his face' (Revelation 22:3–4).

'It is appointed for men to die once and after that comes judgement' (Hebrews 9:27).

INVENTING A SPIRIT

In the early 1970s, members of the Toronto Society for Psychical Research decided to try to 'create' a spirit. They invented a character called Philip, who lived in the days of Oliver Cromwell, and gave him a life story including a real home (Diddington Manor in England). They hoped Philip would 'materialize'; he never did, but instead began to communicate fascinatingly detailed information about himself by table rapping. The information was not self-contradictory, and rarely anachronistic; indeed, 'Philip' corrected the sitters on matters of historical fact. In public demonstrations he made a table rise up a flight of steps on to a platform. 'Philip' has now been 'killed off'. Was he simply a collective fantasy of the group, or did some real but fraudulent spirit power take over the persona which the group had conveniently prepared for it?

SPIRITUALISM

'The scenes of happiness all around us, beautiful white and coloured structures, and the unbelievable colour effects. The placid lagoons, the luscious green meadows and the beautiful colourings of the bird life; and enveloping it all the peaceful, calm and happy atmosphere.' This is not a holiday brochure. It is a description of the 'Other Side' to which Spiritualists say we go after death. And it was given through a medium by a 'departed' spirit.

Spiritualism began in a tiny wooden shack in Hydesville (see Introducing Mysteries), and at first its adherents were treated with scorn. But Leah Fox received the message, 'Dear friends, you must proclaim this truth in the world. . . When you do your duty God will protect you and good spirits will watch over you.' Within two years there were 100 mediums in New York City alone. And since then Spiritualism has grown into a massive international religious organization.

Most Spiritualists treat Christ simply as a 'great exemplar', a master psychic, but 'Christian Spiritualists' also recognize him as God. However, none of the varieties of Spiritualism can really be called Christian. The movement contradicts the Bible's teachings crucially: it discounts the teaching that human sin creates a barrier between men and God, and therefore does not believe in a judgement after death. It relies primarily upon dubious spirit data rather than the Bible; where there is a conflict of view, the spirits are trusted and the Bible neglected.

arm; and some mediums claim to have successfully 'materialized' spirits, who will then walk around the seance and shake hands.

How much does all of this prove? First, there is a great deal of deceit in the history of spiritualism. Many 'materialized spirits' have proved to be simply the medium's accomplice; much 'ectoplasm' to be just cheesecloth or muslin. Not one inch of 'ectoplasm' has ever been examined in a laboratory. Second, many astounding feats can be explained as telepathy or group fantasy. The ouija board at a seance in Flushing, Holland, some years ago spelled out the words of an English poem; later it was found that a young boy across the street had been learning the poem, concentrating on each phrase in turn, for his homework. A Canon Douglas received messages at a seance from his dead chauffeur, Réallier, which contained all kinds of accurate detail—but Réallier was still alive at the time. Presumably the medium had picked up information telepathically from a living brain— Douglas's or Réallier's.

FLYING SAUCERS

Little green men in spaceships used to be a subject for jokes. But today scientists are taking the subject rather more seriously.

One day Antonio Villas Boas was out driving his tractor on his Brazilian farm when he saw a strange egg-shaped craft landing near him. He panicked and began to run, but was captured by the craft's occupants—alien beings about 5 ft 4 in/ 1.6 m tall. Taken aboard, he was made to submit to blood letting, scientific examinations, and even an act of sexual intercourse with an alien blonde. Afterwards, they allowed him to go, and returned to the skies. The next day he developed a complaint which looked very like radiation sickness.

Antonio's story is a typical (if dramatic) example of the thousands of Unidentified Flying Object stories which have proliferated since Kenneth Arnold, a Chicago businessman, reported the first modern 'flying saucer' sighting in 1947. Nowadays the Center for UFO Research in Illinois receives about 100 reports each night.

Are we alone?

French astrophysicist Jacques Vallée estimates that if the reports are reliable there may have been as many as 3 million UFO landings in the last 25 years. This poses a problem. Ian Ridpath has calculated in *New Scientist* that even if there are a million other civilizations in our galaxy, all launching one starship annually, we could expect to be visited only once every 10,000 years.

And we do not know that there are any other civilizations. The often-quoted Green Bank Formula, which suggests that there may be many others, depends totally upon guesswork about one vital factor—the length of time during which a civilization could send out interplanetary communications.

Theories about other civilizations depend on the assumption that there are other planets for them to come from; and most stars are too far away for us to be sure. Spotting a planet at such distances is like trying to spot a pea 27,000 miles away.

Our civilization makes noises (televison signals, radio messages, and so on) which can be heard vast distances away across space. We have never heard anything intelligible coming back. As a result, Dr Iosef Shklovskii, who in the sixties claimed that there were millions of inhabited planets, now declares dogmatically, 'We are alone in the universe.'

Some early UFO reports were clearly hoaxes; there were photographs of upturned soup plates and vacuum cleaner canisters, passed off as 'flying saucers'; there was information about conditions on Mars and Venus which we now know to be untrue; there were reports of craft which could never have got off the ground. Other stories are more difficult to explain. Some may be wish fulfilment. Some may be produced by the 'collective unconscious' (see *Glossary*). Others may be spiritual phenomena.

Is this a flying saucer? The photograph was taken by George J. Stock in New Jersey, USA, on 29 July 1952.

Air Marshal Sir Victor Goddard believes that 'the materiality of a UFO is para-physical', and this is borne out by Lynn Catoe's bibliography of UFO literature for the US Library of Congress. She remarks that much of the literature 'is closely linked with mysticism and the metaphysical' and recounts 'alleged incidents that are strikingly similar to demoniac possession and psychic phenomena'. It is entirely possible that some UFO encounters may be occult happenings on a par with materializations and demonic activity.

HOAXES AND IMAGINATION

Imagination has undoubtedly fostered many UFO stories. In the nineteenth century a mysterious 'airship' was sighted flying over many states of America (with its inhabitants on occasion singing *Abide with Me*!) and was described in detail in many newspapers. From the accounts, we can see quite clearly today that no such craft could ever have flown— especially between planets. The descriptions represented what people in a pre-aircraft age imagined a flying ship *might* look like.

A few years ago astronomer Patrick Moore sent a hoax letter to his local newspaper claiming to have sighted a spacecraft—and to his horror over 20 other readers wrote in confirming that they too had seen it!

WHERE COULD THEY COME FROM?

Which planet could UFOs come from?

Venus? The surface is too hot (800°F/425°C) to sustain life as we know it.

Mars? The 1969 Mariner probe seems to have eliminated all hope of discovering life there.

Jupiter, Uranus, Saturn, Neptune? Too cold, with very different gravitational characteristics.

Pluto? Extremely cold and in perpetual darkness.

Mercury? Too close to the sun to support life.

Outside the solar system? The distances are too great to allow extensive contacts.

Another planet on the far side of the moon? Astronomically impossible.

This forces believers to make one of two unprovable assumptions about 'ufonauts'.

● They do not have carbon-based bodies like ours, but are constructed according to a totally unknown principle.

● They can travel at speeds faster than light without disintegration.

CLOSE ENCOUNTERS

The composer Stockhausen claims that his music comes from the star Sirius B. Has a remote African tribe been in touch with the same star?

On a Saturday morning in March 1954, Mr George King of Maida Vale, London, was in his bed-sitter washing dishes. Suddenly a voice boomed, 'Prepare yourself. You are to become the voice of Interplanetary Parliament.' He dropped a plate.

George King had had no previous links with Interplanetary Parliament, but he did have a family history of psychic interests and a spare-time interest in yoga. Now he found himself being controlled by an entity who called himself 'The Master Aetherius', and said he was a Venusian spokesman for the Saturn-based Parliament, which had selected King to alert the world to its cosmic responsibilities as a member of the solar system.

Today the Aetherius Society, still listening to revelations from the skies, has spread world-wide. Messages come now through a variety of contacts, including surprisingly Jesus himself. According to the Aetherius Society, Jesus is living at present on his native planet of Venus, and claims to be 'one of the Great Masters', but not the Son of God.

Encounters today

The Aetherius Society is simply offering the fascinations of spiritualism (see *Contacting The Dead*) in a science fiction guise. But many other people have claimed outer-space contacts. In the fifties, one American woman even sued successfully for divorce on the grounds of her husband's admitted adultery with Miss Aura Rains—a Venusian friend.

The fashion was set in 1953 by George Adamski's claims (in *Flying Saucers have Landed*) to have talked to a long-haired Venusian in ski-pants. Adamski's evidence, and especially his photographs, are now generally regarded as bogus, but he retains a following, and at the time he caused a sensation.

Stories of UFO contacts seem to have little factual evidence to back them up. For example, no one has ever produced an indisputably extra-terrestrial artefact—even a key-ring or Coke can. Stories of contacts probably have one of three origins: wish fulfilment; occult manifestations (see *Flying Saucers*); or apparitions created by

some 'collective unconscious' process, and received by someone psychically gifted or vulnerable (see *Ghosts and Apparitions*).

Encounters in history

Recently it has been claimed that the Dogon tribe in Mali traditionally possess an amazing degree of astronomical knowledge about a small star, Sirius B, which was not even photographed until 1970; and that this proves a landing of extra-terrestrial amphibians in the Persian Gulf area at the dawn of our civilization. The evidence offered is not at all conclusive, although some mystery does remain. It is also claimed that Jonathan Swift must have had 'inside information' when he claimed in *Gulliver's Travels* that Mars has twin moons. Not at all; he was merely echoing a speculation of the astronomer Kepler's, which was certainly not based on close encounters of any kind.

Members of the Aetherius Society believe that through contact with extra-terrestrial beings they are performing invaluable services for world peace and survival. Their leader, George King, has blessed 19 'sacred mountains' in the world and organized projects such as storing up 'prayer power' for use in times of emergency.

TELLING THE TALE

The most famous UFO contact story is that of Betty and Barney Hill, an American couple who under hypnosis gave an outstandingly detailed account of abduction aboard a flying saucer (apparently such a terrifying experience that their conscious minds had subsequently blanked it out). Their stories agreed with one another.

However, it has to be remembered that we are not certain about how hypnotism affects the mind, that there is often a good deal of convincing circumstantial evidence in 'regressions' to 'past lives' and in seances (see *Life After Life* and *Contacting The Dead*), and that one mind may well act as the 'control' in a shared apparition (see *Ghosts and Apparitions*). It is possible that one of the two fantasized the experience and transmitted it telepathically to the other. Psychological factors in the case suggest that the fantasy would have been a subconsciously attractive one; and stranger things have happened.

ARE WE ALONE ON EARTH?

Human beings have always fantasized that there might be a secret race of beings living on earth beside us. Belief in fairies, for instance, has persisted down through history. Scholars nowadays dismiss fairy legends as one of three things:

● A corruption of old superstitions about ancestral spirits.

● Primitive beliefs about the elemental spirits of nature.

● Folk memories of the original inhabitants of the country who were driven into hiding by invaders.

But Air Chief Marshal Lord Dowding, who investigated hundreds of reports, came to accept that there was sufficient evidence for an unbiassed person to believe in fairies. It seems likely, however, that fairy experiences boil down to an amalgam of 'ghost imprintings' on an area (see *Ghosts and Apparitions*), poltergeist activity (see *Mindforce*), and wishful thinking or make-believe.

Modern-day fantasies of unknown races, such as the 'men in black' who sometimes threaten UFO observers, are probably updated versions of the old fairy theme. It is interesting that UFO sightings are nowadays heavily reported in areas where in previous centuries there were tales of fairy contacts.

WAS GOD AN ASTRONAUT?

Scientists have discredited almost all his theories. Yet Erich von Däniken still finds an enormous following for his ideas. Is he a charlatan or a persecuted crusader?

Von Däniken's theories about visits from spacemen are based on scattered evidence from around the world. For example, he claims that this ancient Japanese sculpture is clearly wearing spacemen's goggles.

Erich von Däniken at the site of the ancient Tiahuanaco civilization, which he dates variously as originating in 1000 BC and 600 BC. Radio-carbon dating consistently gives a date of AD 800.

In 1967 a Swiss hotel manager published his first book. Within five years it was a best-seller in 26 languages, had been turned into a successful film, had inspired hosts of imitations, and had made its author very wealthy. Its claim: that the 'gods' of the past were actually astronauts.

Erich von Däniken's book, *Chariots of the Gods?*, was not propounding an original theory; it had been advanced by others before, including Louis Pauwels and Jacques Bergier, and probably originated in a minor work by Maurice Jessup in 1953. But von Däniken was the first to make it popular. He was writing at a time when Westerners were losing their faith, both in traditional religion and also in science's ability to solve the world's problems. A new, scientific religion, which held out some hope, seemed to be needed. The was-God-an-astronaut theory was ready-made for the purpose.

Stating the exact theory is difficult; von Däniken abruptly changes it, with conflicting claims, from book to book (he has now written six). Basically, he seems to believe that the human race was programmed with intelligence by a race of space visitors (who thus 'created' us 'in their own image' from unintelligent hominoid material); that the Bible and other religious books contain garbled accounts of our contacts with the space visitors; and that the solution to our human problems will be to make contact with our creators once again.

Problems in the theory

The evidence von Däniken presents is contradictory and slipshod. Figures are wildly inaccurate, place-names are misspelled, geographical locations are confused. He claims that our knowledge of history for the last 2,000 years is acceptably accurate; then he dismisses it when talking about South America. In different books he dates the Tiahuanaco ruins at 1000 BC and at 600 BC (the actual date should be AD 800).

He blithely ignores problems for his theory, and relies on several false claims. *Every single statement* in one paragraph about the Great Pyramid, and in another about the New Testament, is absolutely untrue. Four months after publishing *Gold of the Gods*, which contains an account of his tunnel explorations in Ecuador, he admitted that he had never been within a hundred miles of the site.

There seems no evidence for, and much against, his theory. To state just one problem: if *we* could not have evolved to our present state of intelligence, or been created that way, what of the astronauts? Who created them? And who created *their* creators. . .?

'It's true,' he admitted to *Playboy*, 'that I accept what I like and reject what I don't like, but every theologian does the same.'

Obviously von Däniken's theories totally contradict the facts of Christianity. But sadly, this contradiction seems to stem from a total ignorance of what Christianity is. He pictures Christians as devout bewildered people struggling to read ideas into obscure manuscripts. He has no awareness that the message of the Bible is plain, reliable and makes sense as it stands, nor that Christians claim to enjoy a life-giving personal encounter with the real Creator of the human race.

WAS GOD A MUSHROOM?

Another fanciful account of the origin of Hebrew religion which has become popular recently is John Allegro's 'mushroom myth'. Allegro, lecturer in Biblical Studies at Manchester, and an authority on Sumerian languages, claims that by tracing Hebrew words back to their origins it is possible to see that Israelite religion (and original Christianity) was derived from a secret fertility cult. The cult was based on the consumption of the drug *amanita* which comes from a certain mushroom. The New Testament, he says, is full of coded references enshrining the secrets of the cult. However, there are one or two small problems:

● We do not know that the drug ever grew in Palestine.

● The whole theory depends on the idea of a linguistic exchange between Indo-European and Semitic languages, which seems implausible; it also assumes that words *always* retain their original meanings, which is not true.

● Allegro ignores the Old Testament's absolute hostility to fertility cults.

● He offers no explanation of the dynamic life of Christians (unaided by mushrooms) down the centuries and today.

All in all, the theory does not seem to be taken seriously by anyone but John Allegro himself.

Von Däniken claims that the huge statues on Easter Island could only ever have been made by advanced spacemen. But in 1956, the explorer Thor Heyerdahl and seven helpers easily carved a new statue in three days, using only stone tools!

EVIDENCE FOR FAITH?

Miraculous events have often been presented as evidence for faith in God. But do they really prove anything?

The most recent American study suggests that the Turin shroud is in fact a fake. But there are plenty of people who think that this is the face of Christ.

Outside a church in the French town of Arles-sur-Tech is a marble sarcophagus which weeps. There are no apparent reasons. It is not condensation; nor is there a spring in the neighbourhood. Yet it keeps suddenly producing water. Its usual output is up to two pints a day, although in the past it has produced many gallons at a time.

In a chapel by Naples Cathedral lies a reliquary containing the blood of St Januarius, martyred in AD 305. As one would expect, by now it is blackened and solid—except in May, September and December, when at certain religious feasts the contents magically liquefy and look like fresh blood.

Over the high altar in Turin Cathedral, in a silver chest behind two iron grilles, lies a piece of cloth which many people believe to be the actual burial shroud of Jesus Christ. Dr Max Frei, a criminologist, has studied the pollen grains found on the shroud and believes that it must at some stage have really come from Palestine. Upon the cloth are faint imprints showing the outline of a naked Jew's body, as he would have been laid out in death. The wounds in the body are consistent with the wounds Christ suffered on the cross. The mysterious marks do not seem to have been painted on.

But this theory involves incredible assumptions, for the evidence for the resurrection is one of the strongest parts of the Christian church's case for its claim that Jesus is alive today. From the facts we know, it seems impossible that any other theory (for example, that the Romans or Jews removed the body, that grave robbers took it, or that the disciples stole it) could be true. Lord Lyndhurst, one of Britain's greatest ever legal minds, commented, 'I know pretty well what evidence is; and I tell you, such evidence as that for the resurrection has never broken down yet.'

Moreover, there is no good medical evidence to show that the shroud *does* suggest continuing life. If the shroud fails to prove the resurrection, it fails to disprove it, too.

What does it mean?

Is any of this evidence for the truth of Christianity? Probably not— although the shroud has convinced some sceptics (including Ian Wilson, writer of a best-selling book on the shroud) that Jesus was the Son of God. In the case of the French sarcophagus, it seems more likely that there is a natural explanation which as yet we do not understand.

The miracles which Jesus performed were not arbitrary, meaningless party tricks, but were each performed as 'signs' with a definite purpose. In a lesser way, the same seems true of St Januarius' blood; when the faithful are not quite faithful enough, the liquefaction fails to happen, as a warning. This suggests the involvement of extra-sensory powers in the process.

The shroud, if it is a fraud, is impossible to explain. There is striking evidence to support its claim. But serious questions remain unanswered—we do not know much about its history, for one thing. If the early church preserved it, it seems remarkable that they said so little about it. And on the evidence of the shroud, Jesus' body was not washed before burial—which appears to contradict the account in John's Gospel. Ian Wilson has answers for each of these points, but some doubt must remain.

A few years ago 'John Reban', alias 'Hans Naber', a writer of uncertain credentials, claimed that the bloodstains on the shroud proved that the body was not actually dead. After all, corpses do not bleed. Thus, presumably, Christ revived in the tomb and later made his escape. This theory has recently been revived by Rodney Hoare, who believes that the guards placed at the tomb decided to rob it, and that Jesus' followers removed his body and nursed him back to health.

STIGMATA

Clemente Dominguez is a heretic, according to the Roman Catholic Church. But the self-styled 'Pope of Seville'—an ex-insurance clerk who rules his followers from a green corrugated plastic 'Vatican' in Andalusia—has several hundred devoted adherents world-wide, who believe implicitly in the sanctity of their chain-smoking Pope. One of the reasons is that since 1971 he has occasionally experienced 'stigmata'—real wounds, corresponding to the wounds of Christ, which magically appear on his forehead and chest.

Stigmata have appeared sporadically in church history since the thirteenth century, and several cases have been recorded this century. But the Catholic church has always manifested a healthy scepticism; even the most famous stigmatic this century, Therese Neumann of Konnersreuth, was disowned by the church 12 years after first exhibiting the wounds. Auto-suggestion seems the most likely cause of some stigmata, because the wounds often appear where Jesus' wounds were traditionally thought to have been—for example nailprints in the hands—rather than where they would have been—in this case on the wrists. And the possibilities of fraud are vast.

OUR LADY OF FATIMA

On 13 May 1917 a ten-year-old Portuguese peasant girl, Lucia dos Santos, was tending sheep with her cousins Francisco and Jacinta when suddenly a lady appeared to them and announced that she was 'the Lady of the Rosary'. She continued to appear before the children every month thereafter, always on the thirteenth, except in August when she materialized on the nineteenth. The children had been interrogated and threatened by the civil authorities, but their stories had aroused a great deal of curiosity, and in the August vision the Lady promised 'a great miracle' for October.

Consequently, on 13 October there were about 70,000 in the crowd when the Lady appeared once again to the children. This time she announced herself as the Lady of the Rosary and asked for a chapel to be built in her name. Simultaneously, the crowd of adults witnessed 'a miraculous solar phenomenon': the sun seemed momentarily to be falling earthwards.

Although the visions were accepted in 1930 as appearances of the Blessed Virgin Mary by the Roman Catholic authorities, other Christians are sceptical about them. For one thing, the Bible never directs that Mary is to receive worship in her own right, and never suggests that she was in fact specially venerated by early Christians. For another, some of the utterances of the Lady seem to contradict the teachings of the Bible. Finally, the Fatima episode is too vulnerable to other explanations—mass hysteria, collective apparition and so forth—to be intrinsically convincing.

WHAT DOES IT MEAN?

*Exotic, extraordinary, fictitious, true? Can anything conclusive
be said about the world of mysteries?*

Some of the information in this book is almost
certainly wrong. Exploring mysteries is a tricky
business, and there are many pitfalls for the
unwary. Fraudulent claims abound. Sometimes
psychics start faking results because of the
pressure of success; audiences expect results, and
when none are forthcoming, the temptation to
maintain one's reputation with a little imposture
can be hard to resist.

Fraud, conscious and unconscious

Arthur Ford, one of the leading mediums of this
century, had a weakness for alcohol, and is known
to have falsified some effects when most under
pressure. As a result, it is almost impossible to
assess the true worth of his career.

Sometimes faking occurs subconsciously.
Medium Eusapia Palladino, who undoubtedly
cheated occasionally, asked Professor Lombroso,
'Watch me or I'll cheat; John King makes me do
it'—John King being her control spirit. On the
other hand, the enemies of paranormalists have
sometimes planted evidence to incriminate their
psychic investigatees. Even the great Houdini
may have 'framed' psychic Margery Crandon.

Confusingly, often those who are duped like it,
and go to amazing lengths to convince themselves
that the phenomena are real. William Roy was a
spiritualist fraud who confessed his crimes in a
five-part newspaper series in 1958. Ten years
later, he was exposed again, working under the
name 'Bill Silver'—and it turned out that some of
his followers knew he was Roy, yet trusted him
nonetheless.

Unexaminable evidence

Some phenomena are impossible to 'prove' in a
scientific sense. Lobsang Rampa, for instance,
who claimed to be a Tibetan lama and wrote best-
selling books of occult lore based on his
biography, was revealed by a Sunday newspaper
to be in actuality Cyril Henry Hoskins, an ex-
plumber from Weybridge. 'Rampa' immediately
claimed to have swapped identities with Hoskins
via astral travel. And who can prove he didn't?

But the biggest problem in paraphysical
research is 'resistentialism'. This term describes
the peculiar habit that psychic phenomena have
of resisting examination by researchers.
Spectacular PK powers suddenly vanish when the

sensitive goes into a laboratory; UFOs appear at the one moment when there is no film in the camera; ghosts fail to materialize when the ghost hunters set up their equipment. Paranormal phenomena seem to take on a life of their own, rather than following strict scientific laws of cause and effect. As Jacques Vallée confessed about UFOs, 'No matter what approach I take, I can never explain more than half the facts.' It is almost as if a real personality is producing confusing, mischievous results to baffle the researcher.

The magician Harry Houdini waged a campaign to show up fraudulent practices by spiritualists. He claimed to be able to duplicate all their activities merely by conjuring tricks. This picture shows his deliberate faking of a 'spirit photograph' of himself with Abraham Lincoln. However, Houdini himself is thought to have rigged some evidence in his over-zealous attempts to show up other people's forgeries.

Does Loch Ness have a monster? Thousands of people would testify to having seen something in the Scottish loch, but so far the monster, if it is there, has defied conclusive examination. For one thing, the loch is just too vast, deep and dark to be thoroughly searched. But there seem to be other problems, too. One investigator says, 'It's a disturbing fact that hardly any of the original negatives of the better Loch Ness monster photographs since 1933 have survived. Nessie pix are supernaturally accident-prone.'

WHAT DOES IT MEAN?

Is there any way of making sense of the jumbled heap of paranormal claims which confront us? Are we condemned merely to endless speculation, with no sure way of telling the true from the false, the phenomenal from the fraudulent? It is certainly true that simple answers will not suffice. To sweep the whole confused pile under the carpet with explanations such as, 'It's all fraudulent', or 'It's all the work of the devil', or 'It's all tremendous, all a manifestation of the great New Age' would mean ignoring a great deal of the evidence.

Yet it is not impossible to formulate some important principles to guide us in our explorations. These are some of the points which seem to me most crucial.

Unreliable data?
Deceptions take place, and it would be naive to ignore the fact. Serious research into the paranormal must be based upon reliable, tested data—not wild third-hand claims in popular paperbacks, which is unfortunately the source of many people's opinions of the paranormal world. There is not currently enough of this data available to warrant a hundredth of the confident speculations advanced by sensationalist authors.

Christopher Evans has traced how mythical claims of UFO sightings reappear in paperback after paperback—because none of the authors bothers to check with the original source. *Alpha* magazine has researched the famous story of 'Lord Dunsany's ghost', celebrated in hundreds of popular ghost books, only to find that there is no foundation to it whatsoever. It is vital that our opinions should be founded upon established fact, not distortions—whether the distortions are caused by inaccurate reporting, wilful fraud, psychological compensation, or interference by mischievous spirit powers (a possibility which must not be discounted).

Normal laws
Some 'paranormal' phenomena are really 'normal'; we just don't understand the laws governing them. Falls of fish from the sky, spontaneous combustion, ley lines and dowsing— these things *could* be simple manifestations of scientific principles on which we haven't yet stumbled. If so, to condemn them without investigation would be to fall into the error of the 'conservatives' who attacked Galileo and Copernicus for their genuine scientific explorations.

Not evil—but not safe
Some 'psychic' abilities may not be inherently satanic; but this is no reason for justifying their use. Ena Twigg, the famous medium, cannot

It looks like a conclusive picture of flying saucers, but this picture has a completely natural explanation. The shapes in the sky over a Brazilian town are 'standing clouds'—a rare meteorological phenomenon.

remember a time when she was unable to see the misty shapes of 'spirit people'; she believes she was born that way. Matthew Manning had no occultist past when as a boy he began to experience poltergeist manifestations and became a channel for automatic writing. One Christian theory is that psychic ability is a 'leftover' from before the Fall, the time of man's rebellion against God. Perhaps all men once had these powers, but separation from God has ruined them for most of us.

However, since even the best of psychics now possesses these powers imperfectly, and since they are so vulnerable to demonic counterfeit and misuse, to exploit psychic awareness is to open oneself up to unforeseeable spiritual dangers.

Supernatural deceit

Some phenomena suggest that an underlying intelligence may be playing tricks on us. This is what the Bible suggests. 'We are fighting . . . against the wicked spiritual forces in the heavenly world,' it claims, 'the rulers, authorities and cosmic powers of this dark age.' It is easy to become paranoid about demons; but it is only realistic to reflect that if there are *good* supernatural powers there may as easily be *evil* ones. It would be foolish to entrust oneself unreservedly to a force whose origins were unknown.

Beliefs

Many people today are willing to build their deepest beliefs about life around supernatural phenomena they do not fully understand. The Bible, by contrast, invites us into a personal relationship and growing friendship with the God who made both the spirit and the physical worlds.

The proof of genuine spiritual life is not that we are able to perform one or two isolated, bizarre, and usually pointless supernatural stunts. It is that we have made the acquaintance of our Creator by believing in Jesus Christ, and can prove his existence daily in the new purposeful, peaceful life he shapes for us.

We may not know all there is to know about the paranormal. But we can know God, who does. In the security of his friendship we find what years of supernatural experiences will never yield: the true meaning of life itself.

GLOSSARY

Apparition The seeming appearance of someone distant or dead.

Apport Material object which appears to defy natural laws by materializing suddenly or penetrating solid matter.

Asport Opposite of apport; object which disappears from a room and reappears elsewhere.

Astral body Replica of physical body composed of delicate matter, reputedly capable of travelling through space with ease when separated out from physical body.

Astrology Means of assessing the influence of heavenly bodies upon earthly affairs.

Automatism Ability to produce writing, drawings, and music spontaneously, without any conscious effort of one's own.

Cabbala (Kabbalah/Qabalah) Collection of occult Jewish lore, supposed to have been revealed by God to Abraham, but actually nothing whatsoever to do with genuine Judaism. A strong influence on European magicians such as Aleister Crowley.

Clairvoyance The psychic ability to see things or people, past, present or future, which cannot be seen by less gifted individuals.

Collective unconscious Memory traces from former generations of human beings, which may still affect our minds. The phrase comes from the psychologist Jung.

Cryptomnesia Unconscious memory, sometimes released by hypnotism; can be an explanation for unexpected information divulged in trance.

Ectoplasm Strange gelatinous mass exuded from a medium's body while in trance. Opinions vary as to whether or not any such substance really exists.

Extra-sensory perception (ESP) Ability to receive or project information by means other than the generally recognized senses.

Levitation Phenomenon in which objects or persons rise and hover in the air, contrary to the laws of gravity.

Leys Alleged patterns of alignments between megalithic remains and natural features, first observed by Alfred Watkins in 1921.

Magick Attempt to harness miraculous power (as distinct from 'magic', which often refers only to the illusions of stage conjurors).

GLOSSARY